Enterprise Agility

Enterprise Agility

A Practical Guide to Agile Business Management

Gizem Kedici Ozbayrac

CRC Press
Taylor & Francis Group
Boca Raton London New York

CRC Press is an imprint of the
Taylor & Francis Group, an **Informa** business

AN AUERBACH BOOK

First edition published 2022
by CRC Press
6000 Broken Sound Parkway NW, Suite 300, Boca Raton, FL 33487-2742

and by CRC Press
4 Park Square, Milton Park, Abingdon, Oxon, OX14 4RN

ISBN: 978-1-032-21436-8 (hbk)
ISBN: 978-1-032-13909-8 (pbk)
ISBN: 978-1-003-26843-7 (ebk)

DOI: 10.1201/9781003268437

Typeset in Garamond
by SPi Technologies India Pvt Ltd (Straive)

To my son, Kanat

Contents

Preface

Considering the astonishing technological developments in our current environment, life sciences or industries, it is surprising how little has changed in the solid structures of organizations and the way they are managed. However, this is about to change remarkably in response to agility.

Agility concepts rose within the dynamics of project management and soon started to evolve around organizational structuring. Due to the undeniable benefits, a third phase of evolution began: "Enterprise Agility".

Being a business consultant for over 10 years, I have efficiently supported more than 25 companies in varied sectors on their transformational journey through a combination of traditional project management techniques and principles of agile business development. Taking transformation responsibilities in all three stages of agility, in large-scale companies, who are also the forerunners of each phase, along their transition journeys, I have accumulated substantial experience regarding every aspect of agility. During the last years, I have recognized the fast and widespread of the initiative in all sorts of companies, based on the frequent demand for support. I wanted to turn this experience into a book, which would hopefully help many others, who are struggling to find their way through this bold and courageous change.

This book covers all three stages of agility, descriptions of applied processes, lessons learned and realized outcomes, supported with real-life circumstances and company case studies. It starts with the initial phase which is the project agility and describes how waterfall project management transformed into scrum and the positive effects of the change on the project timelines, scope and budget as well as team motivation. Then the second phase of agility is analyzed, which is organizational agility. This chapter mentions the evolution of the agile principles in temporary projects toward permanent organizational structures, as tribes and squads. Then outlines the main components of organizational agility, including possible structures, roles and way of organizing the work. Each component underlines the advantages of transition from the traditional organizational management. For enterprise agility, there is much more emphasis on the fundamentals and transitioning since this state of agility is rather undiscovered and it applies to every functional operation of corporations. This is why the effects of agility on each function are explained in detailed sections (people and culture, finance, marketing, customer engagement, legal & compliance and operations) including the benefits it generates. The last chapter illustrates the enablers of the transformation and how they can help the change to be internalized so that the enterprises achieve assumed improvements.

Acknowledgments

This book is written based on my learnings out of vast experiences I have accumulated through the years. So I would like to thank all my colleagues, with whom I shared both the ups and downs of corporate life. This book wouldn't have been possible without their contribution to my professional life. I would also like to thank the other believers in agility, whom I have been working with or collaborating through the last years, to persuade companies to adopt agility in their organizations. And finally, I would like to thank my family for giving me unconditional love and support.

Acknowledgments

Author

Gizem Kedici Ozbayrac has over 15 years of professional experience; the first 10 years as a business consultant where she has helped companies from different industries transform their business models.

Later, she has held leadership positions in diverse functions and has also lead agile transformation in pioneer multinational companies.

She holds Bachelor's degree from the Middle East Technical University and a Master's degree from the University of Birmingham, United Kingdom. She is also married and has a son.

Chapter 1

Introduction

I have been working in the private sector for almost 20 years, in many diverse roles throughout my career, ranging from finance to sales to human resources, I may say that I am not fond of repetitions so experienced all areas of business, in different sectors. However different my responsibilities were, one year to design a talent strategy in human resources, another year to automate processes in operations, followed by building a P&L model in finance, one component of my professional life never changed: the change itself. Whatever mission I had, I concentrated on changing what I have so that it is improved, automated, altered, fixed, so I had the marvelous opportunity to be in all transformational projects through these last two decades. Although in terms of years it is not extremely lengthy, due to the incredible pace of advancement of technology in all sectors, structural changes were happening in all departments and all processes.

The major trends were firstly digitalization of course and very linked to that process automation, big data and artificial intelligence in the technology area, outsourcing and centralization structures in the operations and finance areas, customer-oriented transformations within sales and marketing functions and finally employee engagement-based programs in human resources. All these trends spread in waves with incredible magnitudes, reaching even smaller and local firms around the globe.

Application and implementation of these sorts of major trends required dedicated project management, so large-scale companies started establishing project management departments and started hiring project managers or business analysts to perform the tasks, similarly also invest in software developers and testers to bring the design to life. Some companies took a further action, caring about the internalization of the changes and established change management units, who work with communications and human resources teams to communicate the reasons for change and ease the adaptation.

As a result, every process, every role, every system changed through the last years, employee inboxes were filled with announcements of large-scale project launches. The two-year-old system was looking obsolete and a task force to improve it was gathered instantly, the mobile applications of companies are redesigned from scratch almost every year with an improved user experience, the job definitions of a function is constantly rewritten to generate fancy profiles. In a way, the demand for change resembles our consumerism in other aspects of life, the more the merrier was the common belief. The only thing that stayed the same through all changes in what we do was how we do it; the way we work, whether we communicate internally or how we organize our responsibilities remained the same and as the pace of change accelerated it became harder to keep up with structures becoming more and more complex.

As those large projects were deployed, in order to continuously manage these introduced concepts, new departments were built (digital, customer engagement, data and analytics etc.). As a result of newly formed teams, the organization widened horizontally, which means more silos are created. Also due to the fact that there are newly established units, the number of employees increased, new management layers formed, just to ensure the new department is able to deliver their targets. As a result, the organization also expanded vertically. This two-dimensional expansion came with consequences: the management of the business became so fragmented that launching a product or generating a new customer segment or even taking a simple decision about a product price became incredibly difficult.

However, at the same time, there is an immense level of change related to the external dynamics: the technological advancements are extremely hard to keep up, volatile market conditions due to startups or new entries or frequent mergers and acquisitions, ambiguous macro environment regarding political tensions, global warming alerts, economic or health crisis all over the world and on top, the customer empowerment with the force of social media brushing off any well-known marketing strategy. It was impossible to keep up with these external forces and yet alone respond to them with strategic actions.

Due to both of these internal and external forces, it became obvious during the last years that this steady type of management, which has not changed for decades, is surely unsustainable. Although the problem statement was perfectly clear, the solution was not at the leader's disposal as a plug and play. Yet there was some light at the end of the tunnel, but it required a progressive approach: agility.

This progression occurred in three phases: project agility, organizational agility and enterprise agility. So this book contains three main parts dedicated to those phases; how they were formed, executed and what were the outcomes. My career coincidentally evolved around these phases, realizing the shift toward project agility as a product owner, then implementing the organizational agility as a transformation officer and finally experiencing the enterprise agility as a business responsible. So all inputs are based on my personal experience with the companies I worked for or many I consulted over the years.

I started my professional life as a business consultant and delivered all those change projects I mentioned above, with waterfall method for 10+ years. Since I was a consultant, I had the chance to experience these changes in multiple sectors ranging from banks, insurance and telecom companies, to retail, e-commerce, logistics and even with public institutions. Since my consultancy company was operating internationally, I delivered many projects around the globe as well. Even though I worked with completely different countries or industries, the governance issues they have faced were surprisingly similar. Agility was originally introduced to our working environments as a project management approach. It was designed to change the universally accepted waterfall method, which was simply a sequential delivery method where the design, development and testing were independent phases. These separated steps were sponsored by different leaders (for instance, the design by marketing, the development by information technologies and the testing by customer services) and caused lengthening of the project timeline, surpassing the project's allocated budget and dissolution of the project goal.

Since I was a project manager back when the agile project management was introduced, I volunteered to apply the technique to an ongoing waterfall project of mine. I experienced the concrete differences of the project flow. So the first part of this book is about how agility changed the way we handled complex change. The initial chapter is focusing on project agility to explain the roots of the developments in this domain. Although I introduce the must-know agile concepts here, I do not go into detail since there is quite extensive literature around this topic. This part also underlined practical points related to project agility, which induced and accelerated the second and the third phases of agility. The final section of this chapter summarizes the benefits of change and how the outcomes triggered the second phase, organizational agility.

After organizations realized the value of project agility, scaling the concept of active project task forces to a permanent structure was inevitable. Since I was at the time, working in a company that had the same ambition, my role as a product owner shifted toward implementing organizational agility. I became responsible for both design of the structures as well as implementation of the new roles and processes. Suddenly, the scale of impact became massive. I cover the interpretation of temporary concepts of project agility becoming the permanent aspects of the organization in the second part, by first briefing the standard organizational design approach in companies and how organizations traditionally managed under these well-known structures. This second section is about how the project specific terms and methods converted into organizational design and human resources topics.

The organizational agility aims to fight the walls of silos and bureaucracy in the organizations. By itself, it resolves a critical number of problems, which I cover in this book in detail. An organization can choose to conclude the transition journey there and still benefit from the new way of working. However, there is a last phase of the journey where the rewards are limitless and the road itself is infinite.

Enterprise agility, which is covered in the third part of this book, is the newest and less known stage of the transformation journey; it is also the most complex and at the same time effective. So I cover enterprise agility in quite detail, supported with case studies from my own experience, from the work I delivered and the companies I have assisted through their journeys, where the details of the cases are altered to protect the privacy of those companies. The main difference of enterprise agility is that the agile philosophy is embedded in each function's operating mechanism. As a result, all departments in a corporate organization change the way they operate. This part of the book includes detailed descriptions of the reforms of each: starting with human resources where every single process is replaced with agile methods, ranging from recruitment to performance management, from career architecture to learning and development. The people section is continued by finance where mostly the planning and control cycle is redefined with a closer look at the three steps: financial planning, budget management and financial control. It is about how agility completely reverse the cycle of planning and target achievement to projecting and closely tracking the business. The third section is about the changes in marketing strategy and delivery; here I link the design thinking and agile ideologies and reflect how they work hand in hand: when the customer insight is gathered, during the marketing communications and finally how the portfolio is prioritized and managed to allow the best use of company resources. The Marketing section is followed by customer engagement, where the focus is to build the customer-oriented go-to-market strategy, how the delivery model should be in order to emphasize the importance of the customer. This section also includes the removal of standard sales target mechanism and motivating the sales team to achieve the promised outcome rather than delivering activities. Finally, the last section describes a better way of internal coordination within the field force. After looking at how the business strategy is delivered, the next section states the supporting dynamics of risk and compliance. Here, the three lines of defense are redesigned according to agility: the internal control, risk management and internal audit. This section is also about reassuring leaders from the magnitude of change caused by enterprise agility, stating how the well-designed lines of defense can in fact enable better control of company risks. The final function of the enterprise agility part is the operations. Since the type of operations differ according to company type of sector, we assume a common operational process, the contact center. Here, I explain the different management approaches to workflow and continuous improvement of service delivery.

The last part of the book is about the agile enablers. After covering the systematic evolution of agility, how the new processes and workflows look like, I wanted to concentrate on what the key elements are supporting this change. These concepts are driven by the lessons learned, the mistakes and the oversights I have observed through the years. The first section is related to the culture, and although it is rather an indefinite topic to handle, I offer certain solid actions that help to build a new culture. The mindset follows the culture, as they are interrelated. A similarly tough ambition, changing the mindset is about supporting the agile behaviors in the organization, creating role models and applying techniques to help the internalization of the new ways of behaving, which cannot be possible without the third section, which is related to leadership. Changing the behavior of the leaders is a shortcut for implementing a new work culture. Leaders are natural role models and if they apply the right principles, many others naturally follow. Here, I give some examples of shifting thinking leadership approaches. Although leaders in the organization are highly critical for the change, they are not alone in this duty. So the next section is about the change agents, which come in the form of scrum masters and agile coaches. Their role in this transformation is explained with specific responsibilities. The fifth section is about the way strategy is managed, since this is a key factor affecting the culture as well. In order to comprehend the dynamics, we focus on the three steps of strategic design: insight gathering, aggregation and prioritization. These subsections help to reflect the serious shift from top-down to bottom-up strategy making. Finally, we end with the change in workflows, in other words, how the companies adapt to their internal governance structures to make sure the flow of information and tasks are conducted smoothly.

Therefore, this book can be seen as a playbook, which can help the organizations, who are willing to embark on the agile transformation journey. The step-by-step explanations of each structure can guide the leaders or transformation offices, whichever sector they operate in. Due to flexibility of the model, there is a selection opportunity for the interested parties; it is possible to initiate the transformation from project agility and follow the steps to further phases, similar to the way it was evolved, or it is also possible to start from enterprise agility and to do all at once. Whichever method is preferred, the relevant parts of the book can shed light on the unexpected journey. I hope that this book provides guidance regarding all stages of agile transformation.

Chapter 2

Project Agility

All transformation efforts in different sectors and different departments, explained in the introduction, had so many diverse scope and approaches but one commonality which was the conventional approach to project management. Over the years, the project management methodologies became so common, you would talk to any project team around the globe, in any sector and would hear similar complaints. The methodology is called the waterfall, and as the name resembles, means the handling of the project in a sequential manner, one activity following the other.

As the below chart illustrates, there are four main stages of project management. The first is analysis where the project vision is defined which leads to agreement on a project scope, stakeholders and timeline. Then the design phase starts, considering almost all large-scale projects include some level of software development, includes defining all the inputs, functional specifications and technical design requirements so that the development can be initiated. In other words, the completion of the design documentation is a prerequisite for initiation of the development efforts. The whole specification document related to the design had to be completed and signed off by the demanding unit so that the development can be initiated. In order to deliver the design without any mistakes before the sign off the business analysts (BAs) aimed for perfection and the business requirements document (BRD) took ages to complete. A similar motive appears when the developers are submitting their codes for testing, where the developers this time overworked on the code to deliver it errorless. The last phase is related to the testing cycle, which can be repeated until the package is ready for implementation. In short, every phase of the project is time bounded and is dependent on the successful completion of the previous phase (Figure 2.1).

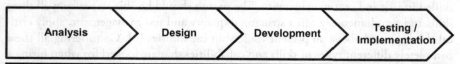

Figure 2.1   Project management phases.

DOI: 10.1201/9781003268437-2

This approach created unknowns about the project and led to ambiguity in management of the project and majority of projects did not meet either length, scope or budget target. So change was seriously required.

Although there are many thoughts on the roots of agile, the general acceptance is that it was initially created with the help of the 2001 Agile Manifesto. It addressed such critical pain points that it was widely accepted by companies of all sizes. These efforts are commonly named as project agility. It is the most well-known version of agility since it is aged and outspread well.

2.1 How Was Project Management Like before Agility?

The role called project management, which is my previous profession, was invented as a consequence of the cumbersome environment a large-scale project brings to the organization. When a top-down defined project was generated at the board level, it was delegated to a project manager (PM), either within the organization if the company has a portfolio management department or to an external consultancy company. The latter usually took place when the project was either complicated that required some outside look or it was highly confidential which usually refers to restructuring or a merger.

In either case, the PM usually exists in the boardroom with a one or two sentence brief, which is in most cases also unclear to the board themselves, of what the project is about. It was later expected from the PM to build the right team that would help manage, track a solid plan, remove all obstacles, measure performance and deploy.

The phases of project management with a waterfall philosophy are first to define the concept, whatever the detail of the brief was given to the PM after the board room, it has to turn into a structural format so that every member imagines the same outcome related to the project. Second, the concept should be detailed down to a project plan, including all the tasks in the breakdown, the risks and dependencies that are assumed, so that the board can see due to which internal or external dynamic, the project completion date will be delayed, and I can claim here that all large-scale projects I have worked in are delayed eventually. Next to the detailed plan, the launch comes with defining the performance indicators and quality indicators which will alert the leaders if things are going not according to plan. When the execution starts, these indicators are closely tracked and reported to the sponsors until the close of the project [1].

In order to perform all these tasks, the PM is required to be a systems thinker and problem solver with excellent communication and negotiation skills, who is also skilled in risk and cost management. The person should be able to perform all these skills and simultaneously run a structured quality and test management, apply critical thinking and above all present leadership capabilities [2]. Considering all these completely different types of skills and capabilities that are looked for when hiring a PM reflects why project management needed to change.

The barriers the role will face are many, some to be noted are:

- *Ambiguity in project scope and expected outcomes:* Since the project was kicked off with a short brief, the unclear scope and underlying topics create a big hurdle for the project team. The above issue is multiplied if even the sponsors of the project at the board level are not clear of what to expect. It is very possible to hear a mumble like "deliver us a working block chain in the supply chain in six months". The reason is in many cases, the solution is what the board is after, rather than the problem. The successful project implementations I have experienced were about resolving a real problem, not ordering a solution.

- *Unmanageable scale of the project:* If, on top of all, the change in scope is too large to handle, for instance, kicking off a cross-functional system change that would start to generate benefits approximately after three years is not very acceptable. Especially considering the lifespans of top leadership roles in international companies, it is highly unlikely that the sponsor will even be working at that role or whether the tool will still be useful. With our current pace of change of technologies, the latter is almost impossible. I have been involved in such a large-scale project which was promised to the top management for six-month completion. I have left the company after a year and three years after they were still working on it.

- *Lack of sponsorship:* The lack of support to the project team may arise from different reasons, first being unclear themselves as listed above, but this doesn't apply to all cases. Another common issue is the sponsorship, not prioritizing enough time and concentration to share the vision to guide the team or to review the work in progress is a common issue. In these cases of lack of sponsor support, a team that is on the wrong path, cannot learn and quickly adjust to what is expected.

- *Conflicts between project team members:* A companywide project (i.e. a new Customer Relationship Management (CRM) tool or a new go-to-market model) requires to involve members from different units of the organization (i.e. Information Technologies (IT), Legal, Marketing, Business analysis etc.) which means employees with different and in many cases contradicting departmental approaches need to align on a project design. These behaviors are generally a result of conflicting department targets and priorities, which makes it difficult for members of departments who come together once in a while to deliver a project.

- *Tiresome business analysis period:* When we consider a project timeline, surely the longest duration belongs to the business analysis. The root cause is that the developers and business units don't have the same vision and approach toward the project and interpreting the business team's demands to an IT language is the role of the BAs.

- *Rework and revisions:* Due to the above-stated issues, the output generated is often subject to rework, in some extreme cases the whole design may get wasted. The sponsor's first review of a tangible outcome is so late in the stage, as mentioned, in some cases after two or three years that there is such a low probability that what is presented serves the initially set requirements well. Naturally, this leads to the project team getting highly demotivated and the following output quality instantly drops. In worst cases, the project budget melts down at the time of the first presentation and there is no room for any correction or improvement. This results in complete shutdown of the project and all involved face negative consequences.

■ *Elongated timeline:* According to research, 90% of projects are finished later than the initial deadline [3]. This is a huge invisible cost to the companies, due to dedicating many internal and external resources longer or failing to launch a product before the competition. The root cause of the delay or even in some cases total cancellation of the project is all the above-listed reasons.

Considering all these impediments the PM needed to overcome, it is clear that the expectation is too high, and it's not realistic to expect a miracle. The impact was delayed projects, missed opportunities, damaged cross-functional collaboration, loss of investment money and time. So it was clear that change was needed.

2.2 The Agile Manifesto

In 2001, 17 software developers, calling themselves the "Agile Alliance", gathered in a ski resort to find an alternative approach to these problems [4]. Although the seeds of these approaches have been planted in different experiments, right after the manifesto started circulating, it really became a trend in technology dominated companies [5].

The speed of adoption is very understandable if we look at the values the manifesto designed [6].

■ **Individuals and interactions over process and tools:** The first value is individuals over systems, and I believe this title deserves to be the first. If we consider the teams connecting for a project, we can easily list three groups of expertise, software development, BA and demand owner business unit. These units are generally located in different floors, buildings and in some cases in different cities. In order to enable communication between these parties, certain task/demand management tools became the main communication tool in the last years.

A business unit member was supposed to submit a task or a ticket depending on the size of the request, explaining a software change, together with the reason of demand and possible effect of this change. The underlying reason was to measure the software developer's performance based on the ticket resolution. It was generally accepted as a well-operating model; however, there was almost no room for real communication or discussing the details of the change request, in order to ensure correct execution. It was highly possible to see a business critical development, being pushed down the prioritization list, and the resolution only came when the cases were escalated.

■ **Working software over comprehensive documentation:** This is another important dynamic since the traditional business analysis was based purely on documentation, generally called a BRD, which is the translation of the business demand to developers. Since this is the only means of description, and all inputs are to be executed with one big deployment at the end of the project, the BRD had to include all possible details.

For instance, in the eyes of the end user, a button click on an e-form is considered as a single step to submit the completed inputs; however, that click needs to be coded in a way that when the button is clicked, all entries are reviewed and based on the rules defined, the decision for submission is made. The definition of this click may take 50 pages in a BRD for a complex process, so it is easy to imagine what the scale would be in a core system change project.

The concept of minimum viable product (MVP) was introduced to replace this lengthy documentation process and define the smallest scope for a working software [7]. The MVP term refers to a product that can be a software version upgrade, a redesigned process or a brand campaign, which means this product is usable with its least minimum attributes. It certainly has great qualities to add; however, with an MVP you can actually test whether the designed product actually works.

There are major benefits related to the MVP adoption; the project team can present certain outputs long before the final deadline and get feedback from their customers so that if things are off the track the rework is minimal. It also lifts the fear of making mistakes which motivates the design teams to be more courageous and to experiment new concepts.

To give an example, a new e-commerce platform which includes dynamic segmentation and an omnichannel integration is an end product, (which can take years to build) where the layout of adding items to shopping cart and checking out is the MVP. So the e-commerce company's project team can first deliver the shopping cart front end to the end users, observe the experience and design the rest of the functionalities in the following sprints. Even if the MVP is not presented to the end customer, it can still be passed on to testers and internal users so that the end-to-end project process is shortened.

The MVP terminology is very frequently used in software delivery; however, it can also mean non-systematic outputs, for instance, a comprehensive and companywide market research study in a marketing department can begin with an MVP of the narrative and questions for a single brand only, then the CMO and the rest of the decision-makers in the marketing function review the output and share suggestions to shape the rest of the framework. In other terms, the MVP is simply the fight against the perfectionism where the 80% pareto logic applies, which means any preparation is sufficient if it answers to 80% of what is expected.

■ **Customer collaboration over contract negotiation:** The contract that is mentioned here doesn't have to be a cross company service contract, it can simply be a verbal agreement between two company departments, to deliver a common outcome. The most typical use of this internal contract is between the developer and business unit: the business member is the customer of the developer because what he or she creates is serving the business unit and eventually serving the customer of the company which they are all working for.

Due to contradicting priorities, these colleagues can easily get into the trap of conflict, as explained in the above section. However, making things harder for one and another doesn't pay out in the corporate life.

So the suggestion is to take the customer into the loop of development to share the progress and similarly the business unit member invites the developer to a customer focus group study so that they can hear the end users thoughts and needs directly. These approaches lift the invisible territory and fuel better collaboration.

A useful tone of communication to achieve this is underlining "we are on the same side" continuously since both parties need to comprehend that dragging topics to rabbit holes help none. Where this communication is not possible, companies try to push both parties to the same vision by the KPI weapon, trying to make the project team participants align on the common goal by leveraging the project outcome as individual performance evaluation criteria.

■ **Responding to change over following a plan:** Large corporations are known for planning. In certain cases, the planning phase is almost equal to the execution. The Project Steering Committees in organizations where all leadership teams review the progress of critical projects are held solely for this reason. Therefore, it is almost impossible for a project team to diverge from the initial agreement. When I introduced the project management before agility, I mentioned the project management cycles which had loads of internal governance tasks that were designed to keep leaders informed and risk minimized.

A typical Project SteerCo presentation might include more than 100 slides and it is filled with project timeline charts, the interdependency matrices (which show the progress over sequential tasks), risk and mitigation action tables and so and so forth. Due to the length of the inputs, it takes about a whole day out of the board member's life and energy. On top, typically, the first projects to be presented face dozens of questions where the afternoon presenters leave the board room in silence and wish they are always arranged for afternoon presentations. So tracking the performance of waterfall projects is both tiresome and inefficient.

Moreover, with the environment we are experiencing, which can be described as volatile, uncertain, complex and ambiguous (VUCA) [8], it is not possible to stick to an unrealistic plan, it will be like hiding a chronic disease which has potential to grow and become harder to treat.

Therefore, allowing flexibility to manage project plans is highly beneficial to all parties involved. We will also elaborate on this topic when we analyze financial management agility.

2.3 Application of Agility to Project Management

Project agility concept is changing the project management theory for good, by shifting the organizations from traditional waterfall project management to agile methodology. The organizations which apply project agility are accepting the approach of the Agile Manifesto and applying the principles to their end-to-end project lifecycle. Adapting agility to a corporation, starting from the project agility is rather simple and easy compared to the others, since it is possible to experience the outcomes by only piloting a small project team and observing the change in the performance. This approach also gives the ability to handle the pilot as an experimental group and compare the performance to the rest of the project teams who are working still with the waterfall methodology. With this approach, the benefits of project agility become highly visible and the scale of adoption increase within a year.

Whichever approach is taken, either piloting or a big bang, there are certain steps to follow: the first action is defining the most suitable teams and communicating the project goal. The goal should be clear and unambiguous and the team should have a belief and ambition toward realization of the defined goal. Since the team will be autonomous in their work, it is very critical for the project sponsor to clarify what the objective is. After that, the team designs the road map of the project and declare which milestones should be achieved in order to complete the project successfully. Finally, the team defines their responsibilities, their areas of expertise and how they can contribute to the project team. I would like to underline a shift in mindset here, first, the team decides the tasks or sub-projects that are required for the project completion, so from day one there is a transfer of decision-making from the leader to the team. Second, the team members define their level of contribution and what sorts of expertise they can support the team with, which means they are free to go beyond their standard job description for the duration of the project and deliver value beyond their profiles. This notion refers to "pull work" instead of "push work", and it promises wider benefits when other agility practices are applied, which we cover in the upcoming chapters.

After the initiation stage is settled, the team starts working on the delivery where the sequential line of project management is not applied, and they are replaced with small time circle output deliveries. All deliverables and project progress are visible to the project sponsors who can observe and contribute.

At the second stage of agility, we explore approaches where the project team is a permanent one, and it's their responsibility to track customer insight and also define their project goals. However, at this stage the organizational hierarchy is still valid so the team is briefed on the requirement and the targeted goal from their leaders.

The reviews of the deliveries are periodically performed with the inclusion of the customers, sponsors and other stakeholders all through the project timeline. This way the team has ongoing feedback for their following tasks. After the completion of the project road map, the team celebrates the success, give each other constructive feedback. They dissolve the team and continue their existing jobs.

2.3.1 Roles

The agile project team is a combination of employees who have the right skills and expertise to support the completion of the project. It is cross functional since large-scale projects include members from different parts of the organization (like IT, marketing, operations etc.). Any member of this team is selected by their representative function heads, and the selection is made based on the specific expertise of the function members. All members of the project are then taken on a temporary mission, which is above their current job descriptions and on top of their daily work.

There are only two specific duties where the owners have to be defined before the project commences. The first is the product owner, which is the role that replaces the old PM role. The product owner is responsible for delivering the project goal. The project road map is driven backward from the goal, toward the main milestones of delivery, (which are the epics), descending down to user stories. The product owner is generally selected and assigned by the project sponsors; however, there are cases where the selection is delegated to the project team. The PO should have an energetic, proactive approach to work, with excellent communication skills and use them to resolve impediments through the project.

The second job is the role of scrum master, wherein project agility, it is not a separate role but an extra responsibility or a hat of a project team member. The SM is responsible for making sure the team follows the agile methodology requirements, that they are productive and the teamwork is highly efficient. They facilitate the agile ceremonies to make sure there is solid progress toward the project goal. The SM in project agility is always selected by the team; however, since this comes as an additional responsibility, the candidates should volunteer for the work. Some teams also rotate the responsibility each three to six months to share the additional work.

2.3.2 Methodology

In the agile universe, there are three types of agile methodology: scrum, kanban and a combination of both, the scrumban. Within the scope of project agility, the first method is applicable so I cover the scrum technique with a project management approach in this chapter, and later in organizational agility, will reflect the dynamic of all three.

Scrum in the scope of project management is an interactive method that enables faster and easy completion of a complex cross-functional project. The project team has clearly defined project goals, the right skilled co-workers to perform their duties and a methodology to follow they are autonomous yet aligned. The method is designed to ensure there is faster delivery of the MVPs, higher interaction with customers during the project and finally higher-quality outcomes.

A case study may help to visualize the concepts even more clearly.

Case: A retail company is aiming to implement a new CRM system with next generation functionalities, in order to enable omnichannel integrated interaction between the brand's retail shops and e-commerce channel. The marketing management is aiming to be able to deliver a seamless customer experience whichever channel the customer chooses. The agile team consists of members from customer experience, insights and analytics, IT and channel management. The member from customer experience is chosen as the product owner due to direct accountability related to the outcomes.

The product owner initially designs the product backlog, on the basis of the epics which will be delivered. In this case; 360-degree customer dashboard as first, which will help to combine all available data sets in a single view, then to integrate the communication channels like having all store interaction and e-commerce data converged to a single platform and a final epic to offer the next best action module. Under each epic, there are user stories that promise an MVP that help build up the road toward the project goal. In this example, the first user story, which is under the 360-degree customer dashboard epic, is related to the customer data mart to be prepared so that a complete view of the customer would be possible. The user story represents what the output will be as the first MVP.

The main difference of a product backlog consisting of epics is the flexibility of time and scope management. This means the epics or the stories may be subject to change through the journey. The only stable factor in this system is the project goal. The team takes actions by shifting user stories along the way, if external or internal factors require it (Figure 2.2).

Although the autonomy may seem like total freedom of activities, the rituals of scrum require high discipline. Scrum works with the help of sprints, which are

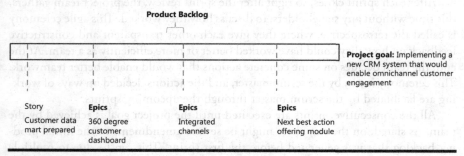

Figure 2.2 Product backlog.

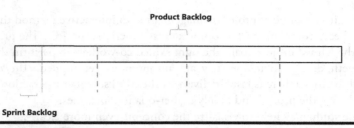

Figure 2.3   Sprint backlog.

time-boxed intervals for the squad to deliver a milestone of their goal. At the beginning of each sprint, the squad selects a sprint backlog from the product backlog and delivers it at the end of the sprint, which is called the sprint planning (Figure 2.3).

In order to make sure things are on track, the team meets daily for a maximum of 15 minutes, which are called the daily scrum or daily stand-ups. The daily stand-ups is a step that is frequently undervalued by the teams during transition, and the first reaction is always a suggestion to eliminate this step. However, each and every team through time accepts the value of time-boxed intervals, so very brief information sharing is very valuable.

At the end of the sprint, the team presents or demonstrates their output to different internal and external stakeholders, which is the ceremony called the sprint review. The sprint review is the most critical component of application of agility since at this ceremony, all stakeholders to the output are invited and their feedback about the MVP is gathered. So although the team preserves their autonomy to shape the design, they do not miss the chance of getting valuable consideration invitations from their customers and stakeholders. At the end of the ceremony, suggestions for the next sprints are also collected to feed the upcoming team planning session.

In our case, the first sprint goal is to create the integrated data design for all the customer data available in the company systems. The first sprint review will be about reflecting the set of existing data in a combined manner. The suggestions collected about what sorts of other types of input can be added or how these sets of data can be best utilized helps the team to get prepared for their next sprint.

After each sprint closes, so right after the sprint review, the project team gathers, this time without any stakeholders, to discuss how they worked. This agile ceremony is called the retrospective, where they give each other transparent and constructive feedback on how they could have worked better or more efficiently as a team. At the end, the team decides on some concrete actions that would enable better teamwork. This ceremony is run by the scrum master, and the actions decided on ways of working are facilitated by the scrum master through the upcoming sprints.

All the consecutive sprints are executed until the project goal is achieved by the team. As stated, on the way there might be several amendments to the initial product backlog that was generated before the first sprint. This can be due to multiple reasons, for instance, some technologies may not respond to the presumed needs or the team comes up with a shortcut, all done with the priority of achieving the project goal and when the goal is accomplished, the agile project team ends their mission and goes back to their daily work.

2.4 The Results of Change

Although corporations increase agility focus once they agree to embark on this journey, there are some who are hesitant about this change. There are a couple of reasons for that: the leaders accepting to have less control on their plans, fear of miscommunication when there is no documented demand descriptions, worries about not being able to find the accountable body when things go wrong are among them.

For the courageous ones, the acceptance of this model changed how we look at organizations, none of the fears and worries were proven to be necessary and the acceptance definitely came from word of mouth.

When my company introduced project agility for the first time, it was also the first case in the country and among the few in the world, the existing project leaders were proposed whether they would like to try this new approach. Together with the fear of the unknown, the project management office allowed a single project to be converted from waterfall to agile. I volunteered to manage our department's project with agility so that our project team became the center of attention of the others. Whenever we had presented an MVP, we had a quite large and diverse audience that was asking about the benefits of the methodology, much more than the output that we were presenting. The pace and the visible outputs in very short time frames were clearly visible. Soon the company decided to convert all projects to agile management. This was the dynamic of attention internally, however soon after we have started receiving calls and invites from other large companies, asking to learn about our experience. After learning about the process and the experience, they have also decided to set a pilot or directly go big bang with their transformation and the rest was like an electric current spreading all over the country.

What was shared with these interested parties through the initial adoption phase to agility were the benefits that we have been experiencing. The benefits can be summarized in these three bullets:

■ **The right scope and optimized resources:** Having the project inputs adaptable to internal and external dynamics enabled adoption of the project scope to the changing business environment. It became possible to observe significant differences between the initial design and the working product.
   The adaptability is ensured by the flexibility in management of the project. With agility there is no strict output promised for the project but rather an outcome is defined. Although the terms are generally used interchangeably, the difference in meaning is highly important in agility. Outputs are the activities we perform to reach toward an outcome. These outputs can vary depending

on the nature of the task; however, the outcome is much simpler, it is to serve the customer better. An outcome of an agile project cannot be something like "implementation of block chain technology to finance processes", since that is the description of the output, which involves a list of tasks that need to be performed to achieve this output. In this example, the outcome can be "enabling safer recording of financial transactions with external parties" which declares an end state, which will resolve the customer issue about monetary losses due to unsafe financial transactions with external parties. The outcome is a simple set of words; however, it includes the target as well as the purpose within. Concentrating on the outcome eases the adaptability of the project design. The project team can work to find the ideal solution that would secure the financial transactions. The team may start with the idea of blockchain as a supporting technology however can find out on the way that this technology is not supported by financial regulators in the country and shift the outputs toward a custom build solution.

Case: A bank started a private teller initiative, who would welcome the bank customer entering the branch, at the counter and direct him/her to the related service desk. However, due to increasing adoption of digital banking during the recent years, the scope of this initiative is converged into a virtual teller that works on the mobile application of the bank and the customer reserves the related service desk for the appointed visit time. The outcome aims to improve customer's experience during the time spent inside the branch, so whether it is provided with a private in person teller or a virtual teller does not make any difference. The team saw the cost that a private teller would cause and quickly shifted the gear toward a virtual teller during the project timeline. If they had insisted on the initial scope and the promised output, they would have hired new people for this teller role and possibly laid them off in a year, they would have invested in equipment and technology which might end up at the bank's warehouse, which is a losing scenario for all parties involved. So having the flexibility to adapt the trends to business reality generated the right outcomes.

■ **Better cross-functional collaboration and employee satisfaction:** The project teams, historically known with the continuous tension and distant relationships changed. The co-location approach of agility brought different employees who used to work at different floors at the office and rarely met in a project room, which allowed social interaction and coffee breaks.

In a previous experience, we were building a task force to figure out a companywide crisis that was drowning from a very tight regulative deadline. We were working on a multiple floor plaza where IT and Marketing were located on different floors. However, the people we have assigned to the team were in this company for over a couple of years and had been corresponding via e-mail, phone or ticket demand system through those years. The marketing was not satisfied with the pace of IT services, and similarly IT services were constantly complaining about the attitude of marketing teams. So I was a bit worried on the project kickoff day when we were gathering for the first time in our project room. A couple of minutes later, due to awkward silence in the room, I surprisingly noticed that these two colleagues hadn't met face-to-face ever before! Due to working as a unified team, the relationship evolved significantly. After a couple of months, I came to realize that they were finishing each other's sentences in a board presentation.

Another factor that positively affects the employee experience is the autonomy of the project team. When the agile team is gathered, the only top-down message is the project goal. The team knows their common purpose very clearly, and moreover, they are free to arrive at that destination by taking whichever road they may find appropriate. This should not cause any misunderstanding or a complete ignorance of the project by the sponsors or leaders since whichever road the team chooses to ride on, they stop at pit stops to check the car's safety indicators. During those stops, the sponsors have a chance to both review the MVPs and give feedback to the team, in some cases guide them toward a faster route and also to discuss the next steps.

This approach is a win-win for both parties since the project team doesn't feel pressured of tracking and has a constant fear of criticism, and the sponsors don't have the continuous urge to check on the team and feel the necessity to be involved more in their design. The feeling of being at the driver's seat is both a relief from constant worries and a feeling of being the architect of their work. Both of them give immense levels of satisfaction to the project teams.

■ **Faster realization of benefits:** The term agile is usually misinterpreted as being quick where it is about making the right things, faster. The velocity is a result of certain factors, the first is letting go of perfectionism. It is said that perfectionism is the enemy of good and that aphorism describes the path very well.

Once the bureaucracy and heavy documentation were removed and replaced with the MVP concept, the project turnaround time significantly decreased. Every sprint, which refers to the cycle of a team's release of their next MVP (generally two weeks long), pushed the members to shorten the design more and more. Another factor affecting the timeline positively is almost no rework remained, with constant review of the MVPs with customers, stakeholders and project sponsors there is no room left for going back [9].

Case: In an insurance project aiming to redesign core operations process, where I was the product owner, we had two phases; the initial year we started with a waterfall method where through the 1-year period, we have spent nine months for the documentation only and hardly generated any output. When we reached the second year, the team converged to agile development, and we gladly replaced a 200-page documentation of the BRD with a two- paragraph description of our story, the more we learned we even started drawing our design on a paper. This way we were able to provide a working front end in three months only.

Chapter 3

Moving Toward Organizational Agility

Once the project agility was implemented and scaled through different project teams across the companies, the above-stated benefits were started to be realized and discussed. The employees were talking about the positive experience of not being forced to spend months on documentation or even worse to throw that documentation to the recycle bin once the project leaders respond saying "this was not what I had in mind". The sense of self-fulfillment started to flow once their work became reality in not a matter of years but weeks, which increased the job satisfaction of work dedicated employees significantly.

It was not the employees only who were quite content with the outcomes; the leaders of the organization benefited from positive financial effects of money not thrown out and quicker time to market. The velocity created a strength against the competitors who were still struggling with waterfall methodologies.

These positive effects were naturally limited with the scope of the agile projects and after the completion, the members of the project teams went back to their original duties. The positive environment and pace generated were time bounded. As a result, the management raised the questions: what if the positive effects lasted, what if those efficient cross-functional teams worked together permanently. These questions opened the gates for further change, and the next groundbreaking transformation was organizational agility (OA).

DOI: 10.1201/9781003268437-3

3.1 How Was Organizational Management Like before Agility?

Organizational agility resembles an earthquake at the foundational structure of a company. The traditional organizational design of a corporation, simply based on hierarchy, which stood still over 100 years while every notion and aspect of a private company had evolved drastically. To explain the change, it would be useful to spend some time on the known structure, which carries a bunch of issues although seeming very ordinary (Figure 3.1).

The illustration of a classic organization's structure where the lines represent layers of authority beginning from the leadership team going down toward the middle management who are acting like a bridge and trying to manage work through both directions and finally the vast majority of employees as the front line [10]. Color codes represent different functions in the organization. For instance, black is sales, gray is finance and white circles represent legal. The top manager, which is represented by the triangle shape, is function agnostic and has an overarching responsibility in every topic of the organization.

This long-lasting chain of command is applied for all sorts of decision-making within the organization. An idea for a new brand or a product or a team emerges in the boardroom, then the middle managers are given the tasks to execute this idea, who act as a bridge to transfer the task to the front line.

Of course, the three layered and three function illustration is rather a simplistic graphical representation when compared to reality. If we rather look into the below diagram, which is a hollowed-out version of a bank's organization chart with around 10,000 employees, it is easier to reflect the burden of bureaucracy. With all the complexity generated by the dissociation of units makes uniting under one company vision and delivering this vision to the customers close to impossible (Figure 3.2).

As an organization grows revenue, branches, or its customer base, the number of boxes also increase both horizontally, meaning that they add new departments or even functions to the chart (most commonly seen new additions are i.e. Customer Experience, Data Analysis, Digital and Innovation departments), and vertically

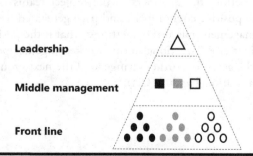

Figure 3.1   Hierarchical structure of a company.

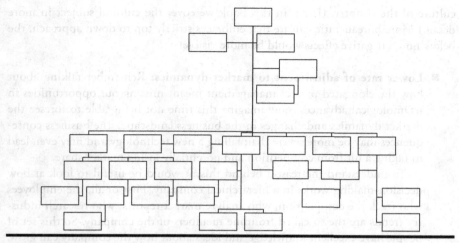

Figure 3.2   A large bank's organizational structure.

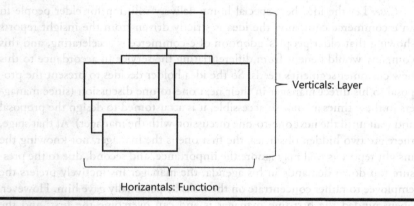

Verticals: Layer

Horizantals: Function

Figure 3.3   Layers.

when new departments need new levels of mid managers to run the topics. The new vertical demands are coming to the Human Resources department constantly and forcing the creativity of the HR specialists to come up with innovative titles for newly arisen layers (Figure 3.3). (Layer: Number of organizational levels having supervisory responsibilities) [11].

Every added layer triggers inclusion of new job definitions, work processes and amendments to the company's Responsible/Accountable/Consulted/Informed (RACI) matrix.

The increase of complexity of managing the single vision within a company generates different sorts of issues. The magnitude of problems may vary in direct correlation with the cultural dynamics in the company and in many cases also the culture of the country. (Later, in this book we cover the cultural subject in more detail.) More bureaucratic culture that embraces strictly top to down approach, the below noted negative effects would be more visible:

■ **Lower rate of adjustment to market dynamics:** Remember talking about how the elongated project management meant missing out opportunities in technological advances, now imagine this time not being able to foresee the market dynamics and changes in the business landscape. The business consequences may be more severe than falling a new technology and may even lead to taking a hit from competition and potentially losing market share.

To understand the reason behind this, it would be useful to look at how decision-making works in a hierarchical company. First of all, the employees who track the competition, who analyze market reports, who research industry trends are the so-called frontline members of the company. So this set of people have excellent knowledge and ideas about how the company can grow. After they come up with a growth idea, they need to present it to their direct manager and try to persuade them to believe in the idea as much as they do.

Case: Let the idea be a special home delivery solution for elder people in an e-commerce company; the idea is strictly driven from the insight reports showing that older peoples' adoption of e-commerce is accelerating, and this company would benefit from differentiating the service in accordance to this new customer segment's needs. So the idea holder decides to present the proposal to his direct manager in their next one-to-one discussion (since managers in these times are not so accessible, it is accustomed to design the proposal and wait until the next one-to-one discussion with the manager). At that stage, there are two hidden obstacles: the first one is the manager, not knowing the insight report as well may ignore the importance, and second, due to the pressure top-down demands in his agenda, the manager instinctively prefers the employee to rather concentrate on the tasks he personally gave him. However, open-minded the first-line manager is and can overcome the first, and the second obstacle is a major driving force.

Let's rather be optimistic about the first-line manager, and regardless of the top-down target pressure, he actually accepts to talk the idea upward, with his own line managers. Even in that case, the proposal has to be carried through the upper layers and repeat the above challenges on each step. More layers there are, lower the possibility of the idea getting accepted (Figure 3.4).

On each layer, the idea is altered or slowly fades away with the low possibility of having all to believe in the employee's insight. The window of opportunity is lost and the company continues to concentrate on what is decided at the board level. This might lead to losing the new potential segment of older customers in e-commerce to a strong competitor in our example case. There is another side effect of the idea generator being demotivated and stopping generating new ones.

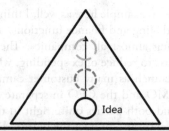

Figure 3.4   Idea flow.

- **Inefficient decision-making:** Another obstacle created by the complexity of governance is the inefficient decision-making. As there are more departments within the organization, the end-to-end lifecycle of business management is more fragmented. If you build a customer engagement department, as an independent unit, when there is an ongoing marketing function, you complicate the customer value proposition process. Now, in order to define a new customer process, two different departments have to come together and mutually agree. As you may know very well, these inter-departmental mutual agreements are not straightforward. Yet, I may even claim that they are one of the most agonizing parts of corporate life.

  Case: I experienced a decision of a 5% price increase on a single product taken in three months. This was due to the fact that the pricing, marketing and sales functions could not agree on the increase. It was a discussion that triggered around the specialist level, which then required their managers to step in, until it became so cumbersome that it was escalated to the board level. The executive committee invited all the related departments to reach the decision which ended up with 30 people in the boardroom, going through a 50-page presentation about what the price should be. The executive committee even asked for more analysis and data, which took another month to complete.

  This example was the routine dynamic of all decision-making and execution in the company. This case can be assumed for all companies having similar bureaucratic and hierarchical structures.

- **Lack of cross-functional collaboration:** The issues related to cross-functional collaboration were described in the project agility chapter. However, their impact in the organizational setting is much critical. The effects reflect themselves especially during a multi-functional project or cross function decision-making. It is rather a daily burden on ongoing business flow.

  The main root cause of this situation is easy to diagnose. The triangular shaped organizational structures are based on targets; which are strict and top down. On the way from this very top to down, the targets are clearly divided into separate parts. Having such segregation involves conflicting sub-targets among departments.

Case: If I may give an example here as well, I think the most typical kind of clash is between marketing and finance functions. These two can be accepted as epic clashes among almost all companies. The reason is that a finance department is targeted to reduce opex spending, whereas the biggest spender marketing aims to launch as many customer campaigns as possible. If you only listen to the CMO and the CFO in separate rooms, after a board-level friction, you may find both parties quite right in their arguments, the CFO has to minimize the costs and protect the bottom line of the company financials, where the CMO has to bring more new customers with the campaign offers, discounts and gifts to the customers to support the top line.

The root cause of misalignment is contradicting performance targets and all this is intentional since the leadership wanted to ensure the optimal top line and bottom line (Figure 3.5).

When the two leaders of these domains cannot agree on the business, it is unrealistic to expect that the finance and marketing department members can gather around a table and agree on the optimal scenario for the company as a whole.

■ **Less innovation or emerging new revenue streams:** The above two topics are certainly linked to less innovative behaviors which has a negative effect on creation of new revenue streams. A struggle on vertical with hierarchy and another with horizontal about engaging with different functions almost kill the spirit of innovation in organizations. What happens in continuous rejection is of course the motivation to suggest ideas to improve business disappear fast.

Another dynamic that blocks innovative spirit is the fear of failure. This concept is bigger than shyness or internal struggles of insecurity but more a systematic culture of creating fear in the organization, induced deliberately. This is induced, most commonly, by internal risk and control guidelines and related corrective actions are taken. It may be result of an employee being laid off from the company as a result of a wrong action. However, this shouldn't be communicated as "take no irregular action in your daily work" since then

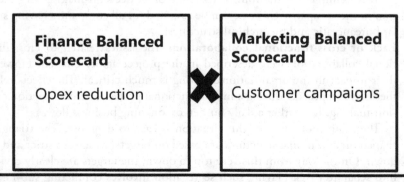

Figure 3.5   Balanced scorecard samples for finance and marketing functions.

employees will consider experimenting or innovating as risky behavior. In these environments, sticking to what is known and continuing business as usual is unfortunately considered safe.

■ **Talent attrition and low employee engagement:** The topic of employee expectations also should be considered in this sense. Talent retention is highly linked to the environment of business management.

Case: To clarify the link to our topic, I would like to mention a previous experience, where we had the task of analyzing employee engagement survey results and preparing an action plan around the negative comments. Although the prejudice among the leadership was that the main identifiers of engagement are compensation related, it was surprising to the board that the top contribution to employee engagement was related to being satisfied with the work. This factor is very reasonable since any individual spending the majority of their time in an office environment, looks for a way to fulfill a work mission, deliver a valuable outcome and of course let others see and appreciate their work as well.

Acknowledging this factor, it can be natural to observe unsatisfied employees actively searching for job posts during their workdays. This is a high-risk item for any business since employee attrition, especially for talents, is costly for the organization. Some of these costs can be summarized as: costs of rehiring including head-hunting and onboarding the new member to the team, the productivity loss and/or service quality during the period of onboarding a new person to the role and loss of expertise the talent carried are some to be noted by Phillips and Connell [12].

3.2 What Changes Did Organizational Agility Bring to Corporations?

The OA concept was formed while searching for an answer to all the bottlenecks collectively. Although there are several theories that link the pathway to agility, the common ground for those theories is the VUCA world [13, 14]. Horney N. et al. explains the concept as, "CEO's are struggling with how best to lead in a VUCA world" [15]. In order to understand the reasons, it would be wise to spend some time on the meaning of the words in this acronym.

■ **Volatility:** A term often used to describe dynamic financial market instruments due to the frequent up and downward moves. Similar dynamics can be interpreted for our business trends today (For instance, the volume of e-commerce demands at the beginning of pandemic, where last-minute curfew decisions caused sudden jumps in demand). So volatility is about the complication of forecasting the future and the pace of change being unmanageable.

■ **Uncertainty:** A business dynamic with lots of unknowns, like a pharma product waiting for regulatory approval, not being sure of the time span of governmental decisions, making B and C plans for outcomes. Uncertainty forces companies in affected sectors to make their decision-making models extremely flexible.

■ **Complexity:** When your business is tied to different channels and sources of data, (For instance a retailer, in order to launch a product, they need to make a different launch plan for each country/channel/segment). The complexities make new business design costly and cumbersome [16]. To better manage the complexity, companies are relentlessly working on integrated platforms to have leaner process management.

■ **Ambiguity**: HBR calls this area "unknown unknowns", which makes data and evidence-based decision-making for companies almost impossible (for instance, a telecommunications company entering a public funded monopolistic Asian market, where there is minimal information and data to act on) [17]. The ambiguity pushes companies to take smaller steps when compared to 10–20 years ago, not to decide on bold actions due to the risks involved.

The incredible rise of the digital age, rising customer power, at the same time data evolving from a reporting tool toward artificial intelligence, and in parallel the manufacturing advances which initiated industry 4.0 started to reshape all industries. So the VUCA environment became the reality that executives around the world had to deal with. This type of world is harder to run and manage considering the issues stated. So change in the way of working for companies was inevitable.

The most overarching action that collectively addresses all above hurdles is OA. No surprise that Oliver Wyman states, in an Economist Intelligence Unit (EIU) Survey, 96% of companies responded that agility was highly important for their companies' future success and more than 80% have taken actions to improve agility [18].

All actions toward agility will help a company benefit for sure; however, the magnitude of change will multiply if all aspects of OA are applied as a whole.

> Agility is the ability to adapt and respond to change ... agile organizations view change as an opportunity, not a threat.
>
> Jim Highsmith [19]

3.2.1 Components of Organizational Agility

Organizational Agility (OA) means building cross-functional teams that can deliver an end-to-end business or process in the organization. That team becomes responsible for bringing speed and responsiveness to change while maintaining business stability.

The concept resembles Lego building where the base platform is the company backbone consisting of structures, sustainability measures, or financial strength, and the bricks in different shapes and sizes are the new business dynamics introduced within the company. If the backbone is strong and stable, the innovative addition of new concepts is welcome for experimentation. The bricks represent the new

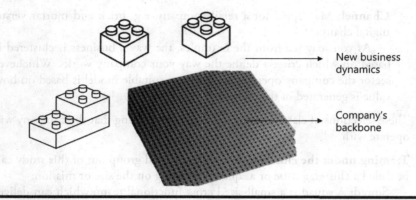

New business dynamics

Company's backbone

Figure 3.6 Company backbone vs new business dynamics.

business which will be brought by the agile business teams, working on developing or improving the business collectively (Figure 3.6).

If the company is rather made up of small bricks, without the platform, which is the base, it is then a startup structure. The startups are emerging small teams of people, gathered around a single purpose, to make their business sustainable. Since they don't have the luxury of this backbone platform, which guarantees a solid cash flow, their existence depends on making the small bricks work well otherwise the whole business will dissolve. Sometimes, during agile conferences, members of audience from startups always ask me, "What you have been talking about is the way we work in our company, nobody has a job description, we all work for the existence of our company and if we don't collaborate we cannot survive" and they are exactly right. Organization agility method tries to mimic a small company's way of working.

What large multinationals have is the stable backbone and an effort to continue their base with the help of successful business strategies. Agile organizations aim to combine both features and create a system where the bricks are built on the platform. So in a way, the agile organization is sustainable as a large corporation and is fast and flexible as a startup at the same time.

- **Classification of the business:** The initial step for transforming the long-lasting boxed organization chart is to drive away from functions and find clusters of business for an end-to-end management. This design should start at the board level, to overlook the whole organization, and define pods who need to collaborate to run and change the business.

  The formation of **business** clusters usually occurs by three criteria:

  - **Segment:** May apply for a bank, e.g. commercial segment and corporate segment
  - **Product:** May apply for an insurance company, e.g. the motor, health and non-motor products

- **Channel**: May apply for a retail company, e.g. brick and mortar versus digital channel

  As you may see from the examples, the way a business is clustered is based on which criteria define the way your company works. Whichever sector the company operates in, the most suitable model is based on how value is generated in the company.

These selections of classifications represent the teaming that the company will operate with.

■ **Teaming under the clusters:** Each differentiated group out of this study can be called a cluster, a tribe or a squad depending on the size or mission:
  - **Squad:** A squad is a small-sized cross-functional team, which can deliver an independent end-to-end outcome. The size can be explained best by Jeff Bezos's quote "every internal team should be small enough that it can be fed with two pizzas". The team should have the autonomy to deliver an MVP and further develop it with the help of stakeholder reviews.
  - **Tribe:** Tribe is a combination of squads, which represents a meaningful standalone business. A tribe should be able to have a dedicated P&L, which means all revenue and cost items related to the tribe's business should be reportable and manageable. Generally formed with four to six squads, the tribe consists of approximately 50–60 employees. As mentioned above, a retail banking tribe may be fit for a bank or a motor tribe for an insurance company, the tribes represent how the business is managed.
  - **Cluster:** A cluster may only apply to a company if the organization consists of over 1,000 employees. In a cluster, the tribes are gathered under the same roof with a common P&L. Typically it appears that the organization is managed under a CEO and General Managers where each General Manager is responsible for a differentiated business. A conglomerate with two major lines of business as energy and automotive can be a great example of cluster type of OA alignment (Figure 3.7).

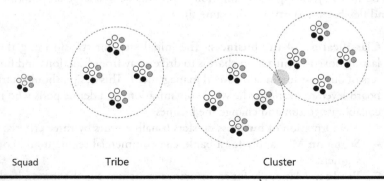

Squad   Tribe   Cluster

Figure 3.7   Agile organization structure sample.

Case: An example structure for all can be an FMCG company which produces packaged food and beverages. The clusters may be food and beverages with two different board-level leaders responsible for each, the tribe under food can be chocolate and the squad within the chocolate tribe can be brand x chocolate bars.

It is more *beneficial* to go with flatter structures as long as the number of employees or the total size managed allows. This way the cross alignment of the cells would be more efficient.

- **Chapter:** A chapter is the preservation of functional expertise in the squads. As the below diagram shows, all these blended teams still have representation of their functional expertise which is crucial to get the job done. The classification of technical skills and expertise within the squad is defined by which chapter the member belongs to (Figure 3.8).

A typical example is product management. Where all product managers in a traditional retail company *report* to the marketing department; in an agile organization, the product managers are assigned to the squad that governs their products. Those members also naturally become a member of the marketing chapter.

The chapter *represents* the common way of working and their goal is to perform marketing tasks in a similar method and philosophy.

- **Roles:** With the new structure, new roles are inevitable but even if you cluster your organization well and form the squads with talents, assigning the right people to the below listed roles is the most critical step of the transformation.
  - **Product Owner (PO):** The scrum guide defines the role of the PO simply as someone responsible for maximizing the value of the product resulting from the work of the squad [20]. That means, every aspect, decision or output related to that product is under the guidance of the PO. When

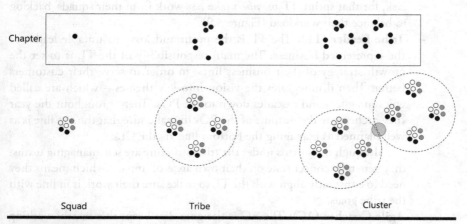

Chapter

Squad   Tribe   Cluster

Figure 3.8 Chapter structure in an agile organization.

compared to the PO in project agility, the main difference is that this role is permanent and full time, so as the accountability to deliver the business.

The PO is responsible for conversion of the product vision to product backlog, which is the list of outcomes that will carry the team toward the desired state. However, orchestrating the team to create the best outcome of the product vision is not the sole responsibility of the PO, they also need to pull suitable work from the backlog and align common topics with the other POs.

What is expected from the POs in OA is taking the responsibility area a step forward. So the POs should have an innovative and experimental vision toward their area.

- **Chapter Lead (CL):** The CLs are the gatekeepers of the functional expertise that they represent. Generally, the CLs are the most experienced and/or skillful members of the chapter so that they can transfer expertise around their area to other chapter members. Depending on the company's size, the CL is also the people manager of the other members of the chapter in that tribe. The people management responsibilities are limited to coaching and functional supporting the team members and do not represent a hierarchy. In order to diverge from the classical sense of "manager", the CL belongs to a squad as a member and pulls work from the backlog apart from coaching chapter members. This rule is important because once the CL pulls tasks from the backlog, others comprehend that he is not a manager but a coaching leader in the team [21].

The CL may also have a certain chapter related backlog, apart from the product related tasks. For instance, the IT CL in a tribe may need to run an annual coding quality assessment for other IT team members distributed in other squads in the tribe. These chapter related tasks are handled in a separate backlog with IT chapter members and when there is a common task, for that sprint, IT *members* take less work from their squads' backlog to balance their workload (Figure 3.9).

- **Tribe Leader (TL):** The TL is the profit and loss accountable leader of the represented business. The main responsibility of the TL is to set the growth strategy of their business lines, in order to serve their customers better. Then disintegrates the vision into key themes – which are called epics in agile – and cascades down to the POs. Then throughout the year they orchestrate the outputs of the POs to make sure that the top line is as well planned as managing the bottom line via the CLs.

Although the squads under the tribe structure are self-managing teams, they generally concentrate on their own areas of impact, which means they need to constantly align with the TL to make sure their work is in line with the tribe goals.

- **Agile Coaches (AC):** The AC is the glue that keeps this matrix working philosophy altogether so that the teams are concentrated on collaborative

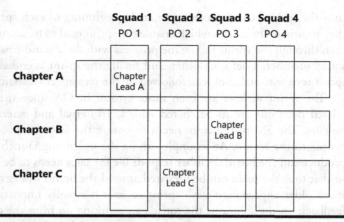

Figure 3.9   Chapter lead structure.

outcome generation while applying an agile way of working. The AC is also responsible for the high motivation and result orientation within the teams so facilitates different sorts of liberating structures where and when needed. These methods are the toolbox of the agile coach when team dynamics or atmosphere doesn't go as planned [22].

- **Scrum Master (SM):** The SM is the second role that coincides with project agility; however, there are certain differences since the term of the team is not temporary and there is a continuous demand for the SM in the squads. Where the AC is responsible for the well-being of the tribe as a whole, the squads may have dedicated change agents to keep things moving according to plan. The SM is either a dedicated member of change force or a volunteering member of the squad, who has good communication and organizational skills. If we simplify their mission, we can say that the SMs are responsible for the "how" where the PO is responsible for the "what".

■ **Cadence of Agile Approaches:** Agile has different work management approaches that can be applied based on the work's nature.

- **Scrum:** Again, according to the scrum guide, the term means: "an agile framework within which people can address complex adaptive problems, while productively and creatively delivering products of the highest possible value" [23]. In my words, it's an interactive method of organization that enables squad members to plan their way toward accomplishing the business or product vision. This method is the answer when there is a business work that allows improvement, change and growth.

As explained in the project agility, the scrum works with sprints; however, this time it doesn't have an end date like the project agility, it is a continuous event that allows managing the business effectively and transparently. The cycle of scrum applies completely in OA. The project team runs the sprint planning ceremony at the beginning of each sprint where they prioritize the stories which enable the sprint goal to be accomplished, then through the sprint follow the progress with daily stand-ups where all squad members brief each other, and finally the sprint is ended with the sprint review to stakeholders, followed by the retrospective session [24].

The sprint reviews are even more critical in OA since the business related decisions are to be shared with key internal and external stakeholders. The SM of the team needs to ensure the attendance of relevant people to the review. An example can be the upcoming launch of a new product and the board member responsible for sales needs to be informed so that the sales team can be prepared around the brand strategy. External stakeholder engagement with sprint reviews is equally important to get feedback on the solutions the squads are working on from the customers or partners to reflect the level of future success of the product early on.

Likewise, the importance of retrospectives needs to be underlined at this point. In project agility, the team learns to work together and it is very important to be able to deliver the goal; however, in OA, the team is permanently tied together under the squad and has to find a way to make it work. Retrospectives are extremely useful in terms of elimination of obstacles or creating a common understanding. In my observations, the major shift is accomplished when the members from different (and previously conflicting) functions start understanding each other's work and their complexities, so start building empathy toward each other. An example revelation I heard came from a marketing specialist in a new product squad that confessed, "I never knew how long and detailed work was required to write a code, however now I see that my colleague from IT function completing all these tasks for a screen change, I feel the urge to help him".

- **Kanban:** The kanban method is a means to design, manage and improve flow systems for knowledge work [25]. The biggest difference from scrum is the keyword in this sentence which is "flow". For works which are not time bound or filled with change activities but rather run the flow, kanban is an appropriate model to pick.

   A major difference from scrum is the lack of a cadence like the scrum model requires. Since kanban is about managing the flow, the only ceremony that enables the management of the flow is the daily stand-ups. The team leverages that time to track their progress on tasks that are under to do or in progress status, considering their maximum capacity. The capacity is numerically justified by a method call work in progress: it can be the number of calls for a contact center or the summation of ticket sizes in a DevOps team. We cover the management of the kanban style of work with case studies in Agility in Operations Section.

- **Scrumban:** As not all jobs can be classified as clear as night and day, there is a method for hybrid type of work. In scrumban, the team simultaneously

	SCRUM	KANBAN	SCRUMBAN
Type of work to manage	Change > 70%	Run >70%	Change 50% – Run 50%
Planning	Work is divided in sprints and MVPs delivered	Work is in flow, team track work in progress limit	Both MVP is delivered and work in progress tracked
Tracking	Outcomes are presented to stakeholders after sprint completion	Performance reports are tracked and quality assessment done	Both measurements are applied.
Example teams	Business squads, project teams	Operations, accounting and sales	Human resources and communications

Figure 3.10 Scrum, Kanban and Scrumban comparison.

plan a change and follow the route toward the delivery and at the same time keep delivering the routine type of work (Figure 3.10).

As the table reflects the differences within the approaches, scrumban is ideal to be used when the nature of work is partly operational and partly about developing the foundational work to shift its base to another level.

An example case would be human resources: within human resources function there is a dedicated team for recruitment, where the team goal is to fulfill the open positions with the most suitable internal or external candidate. All team members have their daily tasks dominated around either screening or making interviews with candidates. All the time reserved from these efforts are devoted to improving the candidate experience with certain projects, like implementation of an automated initial interview system which will single out the most eligible candidates and lessen the interview workload of the recruiters. This blend of run and change activities can be tracked together under the same board and more is done to improve the ongoing work, the less operational activities the teams have.

3.2.2 Requirements of Organizational Agility

▪ **Agile office:** For companies who would want to embark on this journey, the agile office, which is the group of change agents, dedicated to accelerating agile mindset shift is highly necessary. This office is commonly formed by the agile coaches (if applicable also scrum masters), communications and human resources. The main responsibility of this task force is to onboard the squads to be able to run their sprints (with the help of a three-weeks study called Sprint 0, where the squads form their product backlog based on their mission). When the sprint flow starts, the primary role of the office becomes serving methodologies, training and coaching to the squads in order to achieve adoption and internalization of agile ways of working.

■ **Governance:** For tribes to be responsible for their P&Ls and have the necessary tools to manage them, the functional budgets are reshaped as tribe budgets and allocated to the tribes. Typical included items under the tribe budget are marketing, IT, operations/logistics and human resources. The TL reviews the situation of the P&L with the CEO in monthly or quarterly reviews.

So at this stage of OA, there are still the traditional systematics such as planning and control cycles. The tribes are demanded to plan their financials and abide by the top-down financial plan. We see how these shift in the business agility chapter.

■ **Facilities:** In the project agility chapter, it was described that the members of organizations who have not even met personally but have been corresponding on work heavily come together to work in the same team. So the co-location philosophy of agile aims to bring members to the same working area is also important. But this is rather critical for the initial period of onboarding and engaging, sort of breaking the ice. Some thinkers used to claim that the colocation is an unbreakable deal; however, we have been observing that the remote working dynamic as a result of the pandemic is moving us toward borderless digital interaction.

Nevertheless, the work location should be redesigned to allow each squad to work together and have creative areas, to design their work in an open office environment. Many companies who transformed have built special floors dedicated to tribes that look and feel like a startup company with comfortable areas to relax, play areas etc.

■ **Technology:** The technology requirements are the easiest among the rest. The only useful system for squads to manage their backlogs is a workload management tool. Although there are three top providers around the world, the required functionality is rather simple: the team to commonly view a digital board with all their stories and to be able to edit their jobs to be done. This becomes the main tool for the team and key action is entered to the board so that even if a team member misses a whole week, it is easy to catch up with what has progressed. There are also mobile application versions of these tools so even the field staff can log or change their stories from their mobile phones, on the way to a customer visit.

3.3 The Effects of Transformation

The effects of OA transformation can be explained in a similar approach as of project agility. In very basic terms, the same category of benefits applies on a wider scale and in a permanent manner. Nonetheless, it is useful to have a separate look at the implications to further clarify the dynamics.

■ **Employee engagement:** It is meaningful to start with internal effect since the reflection on the team is rather instant. In project agility, we have covered the benefit of co-location and acting as one team during the phase of the project. However here, the effect is constant. In the first model, the teams gather around a common project goal, which helps them to reduce their anxieties around adverse targets. The latter bounds the cross-functional members for good. The targets are set together, and no room remains for conflicts.

   Case: I would like to provide an example case here to illustrate the change. We were visiting a recently formed tribe, in order to hear their thoughts about the transition and collect feedback. One of the squads in that tribe was responsible for large-scale corporate deals, and the developers of the corporate offer screen were united with the account managers of the corporations. One of the developers from the team wanted to comment and said,

> I was working with the account managers remotely for over three years and used to be bothered with the incoming urgent titled emails and relentless phone calls to get the online bid system working. I never knew and frankly never cared about what it meant until last week. Last week we were bidding for a large sum and there were some system issues, I was so running around the floor to get it fixed that my glasses fell!

You may notice his referral as they even became "we" within only weeks.

So owning a common purpose and having the ability to work for it together, without the *borders* of the functions that limited them, contributes to the employee engagement significantly.

■ **Resource optimization:** If we again look at this topic in comparison to project agility, the main benefit of our previous topic is framed around utilizing the time and effort invested in the project in an efficient manner, whereas in OA the resource optimization is driven from both the optimal appointment of members of the tribe and allocate the optimum level of investment to the work where the value generation would be maximum.

   This optimization is granted by the ability of tribes, prioritizing the outcomes which are more effective toward their goals and ambitions. For Rotich and Okello, fluid resources refer to internal capabilities to redeploy resources rapidly. The fluidity originates from mobility of employees, their rotation of jobs and knowledge [26].

The main enabler of fluidity in a tribe is when the POs and CLs work very closely. In a sample flow, the PO in a business development squad comes together with the other POs and CLs, to discuss the new product that is soon to be launched and the number of people required to launch it. The key value is brought by the other POs allowing suitable members to flow to work *and* the CL to support if there is an expertise gap in order to fulfill the task.

On the *investment* optimization level, the PO and the squad are named accountable for the P&L performance of their line of business. So with autonomy comes a huge responsibility of managing the expenditures effectively. The squads are still bound to act within the budget given to them from top down; however, in order to manage their expenses within that cost limit, they try to make the optimal investments.

■ **Time to market:** The third main benefit is also the outcome of a combination of different dynamics in OA. Prioritization of the right outcome for the customer benefit, supported by the fluid and highly engaged teams naturally causes the right level of dynamism to be able to produce more.

The teams then concentrate on the pace as well as the output in progress and when *concentrating* on the speed, the concept of MVP that we have analyzed in project agility also helps immensely.

In addition, if there are obstacles on the way like a vendor delaying their submission or a global unit not approving the product, the critical go to people that are required to solve the issue are already members of the squad.

In brief, removing all internal complexities allows the departments to concentrate on serving their customers in the best and fastest way.

Chapter 4

Evolving into Enterprise Agility

By now you may realize that as the project agility evolved to organizational agility, scale of positive effects of transformation grew in scale. I should note that for the vast majority of the companies who decided to take on the agility journey, the implementation of the organizational agility represents the end of the road, they do not pursue this stage. However, there are the brave ones out there who wanted to push the agenda forward. So in this chapter, we deep dive into their stories.

This chapter is concentrating on the third phase of agility transformation, enterprise agility where all units, processes and culture are affected by the new ways of working. The Business Agility Institute defines the state as "a flow, from the market demand to delivery to customers" [27]. This is a very simple explanation that holds a great deal of change in each and every concept of a company management. It underlines the change of business management so that every move is defined by the needs of the customer and executed by the team who has the best insight and experience, where all the rest becomes functions that enable faster and better response to the customer needs. An organization which is agile on the enterprise level is released from all the standard business management processes and techniques that MBA courses teach and corporations apply.

Due to being the most recent and unusual approach to management, there are only a few companies that apply these methodologies, and there is less literature on them. So I try to cover the topic in much more depth in the upcoming sections. In order to understand the magnitude of change, it would be wise to have analyzed the management trends that exist currently, first.

DOI: 10.1201/9781003268437-4

4.1 Existing Trends in Management Domains

In order to understand how companies are managed before agility, the current trends in different organizational demands would be informative. Classical business management relies on certain functions in the organization, performing their responsibilities, within the borders or so-called segregation of duties given to them. How they perform these tasks are frequently followed and evaluated with the help of balanced scorecards, which are the company performance indicators. The system is so strictly followed that it shapes the private company culture in today's world.

When we look at the main functions in such a large-scale company, we see the below illustrated six domains as a common structure, although deviations may arise due to the sector it operates. There are different trends and dynamics that are currently shaping or changing the structures of how these functions are managed. These changes exist independent of the agile concepts; however, they are all linked to interpretation of enterprise agility (Figure 4.1).

- **People & Culture:** Previously named as Human Resources, the change of the name reflects the future of this function which aims not treating employees as resources that need optimization but rather converging into an enabler of business, with higher concentration on strategic workforce planning, talent programs, employer value branding initiatives. In order to implement these initiatives, people and culture (P&C) needs to be involved in top strategy discussions and business plans and has to explore how to support the business units with the right talent appointments or with new practices which allow a change in the behavior. In order to succeed in this strategic mission, P&C tries to reduce operational activities as much as possible. Common trends are centralizing business partner support via the P&C service centers or automating manual processes.

Figure 4.1 Business domains.

■ **Finance:** The rise of industry 4.0 which brings the computerization of industries, as Forbes names it, includes one trend that is shaking the grounds of finance: Robotic Process Automation (RPA) which is an application of technology, governed by business logic and structured inputs, aimed at automating business processes [28, 29]. What the term means for finance is elimination of the heavily manual activities in core finance operations like accounting and reconciliation. Instead, the finance teams are willing to convert the focus toward getting closer to business, act as a business partner to be able to detect financial risks faster and steer the business units toward a better P&L.

■ **Sales and Channels:** The main trend that is affecting sales departments all around the world is to diverge away from a sales strategy that is based on a generalist push approach. The replacement is customer specific narrative generation that creates a pull rather than a push. The name of the function in some cases even changes from sales to customer engagement. This trend applies to both B2C and B2B2C sectors. The natural outcome of this change is the persona of a typical sales representative shift toward a deep listener with an analytical mind to propose the right solution rather than a fierce dealer who doesn't give the customer the space to speak.

This function is not free from the technological advances that the others are facing since the new customer-facing profile requires excellent digital communication tools and to get access to integrated customer insights which guides them to their next best action.

■ **Marketing and Digital:** As the change of name suggests, addition of digital to marketing function is the biggest change in the structure. Some organizations who invest enough in digital even have a C level representation, Chief Digital Officer, CDO in the board; however, the common practice is to combine the role with the CMO. This is a natural coupling since the main aim of marketing, which is to build the brand communication strategy, can't survive with traditional commercial channels. The product launch discussions have long moved away from billboard or prime time TV to fleet functionality in Twitter or influence video posts on the social media channels.

■ **Operations and IT:** Although Operations and IT is coupled, for technology dominated sectors, IT easily becomes a separate function managed by a CIO who is a part of the executive board. Regardless of the governance there is undeniable change in all subsections of this space. Basically, IT acts as an optimization engine of all operative processes with the ultimate goal of cost minimization. As mentioned in finance, specifically for accounting activities, the operations domain as a whole is subject to the RPA.

Another major technology that reshapes the operations is the internet of things, which is to create a network of devices connected to streamline a process. This will affect the position of manufacturing and supply chain operations in the near future as well [30].

Since automation resulted from the usage of technologies to release operational forces, the workforces are shifted toward services under the operation umbrella. As a result, the operation functions all over the world are shifting away from being just cost centers to service centers. It became very common to see operational workforce having customer satisfaction or even sales targets. Similar to the change in sales, the general profile looked for is also changing toward customer-oriented profiles.

■ **Legal and Compliance:** The least affected function with all industrial changes among all, in terms of structure, is legal and compliance. The trivial reason is of course immunity of L&C from advancement in technology or industry trends. However, the more digitized the risk involved processes become, the duties of the L&C functions become easier and more secure. Audits were used to be based on sample monitoring activities where the auditors had to check thousands of transactions. However, thanks to the advancements in the artificial intelligence space, for auditors, it is possible to investigate not a sample but the entire record with a click. This also enables the auditing becoming a pre-transaction alert rather than a post-event control.

As we can see from the above descriptions of aspects of change in each function, there are a number of external effects like digitalization and industry 4.0 as well as new players in the sectors like startups and tech companies. At the same time, the customer becomes more and more powerful with access to all sorts of information and is able to give more informed decisions as well as demand a personalized service. Also, specifically in some markets or regions, there is high turmoil in the economic and political environment, which raises concerns on how effective the financial management is. In brief, all those external factors verify the VUCA environment we have described in introduction to agility.

The most critical point to underline here is that there is often a false assumption that the changes are all-around technology, and there will be minor effects on other business units in the organization. If the only department that needed to follow the trends was IT, then our initial phase of agility in project management would be sufficient to manage all very well. However, since almost all existing management processes in a wide range of sectors are not able to keep up with the pace of change, the need for systemic change seems inevitable. Although there are multiple methodologies that help organizations to cope with functional dynamics, there is not one so holistically refreshing all business units as enterprise agility. Next, we will deep dive into each unit and describe their effects.

4.2 Evolution of Each Business Domain with the Agility Effect

In this chapter, each main management function of organizations is analyzed in order to understand the current way of working, the issues and what changes arise with enterprise agility. These sections can be interpreted as a checklist for companies who are planning to embark on this transformation journey. Although there are clear differences around sectors or markets, the general concepts apply to the majority. Each functional statement of agility is supported with case studies to reflect the real-life experiences.

4.2.1 Agility in People and Culture

It is rather rational to start analyzing the effects of agility on company domains from the P&C perspective. The obvious reason is that the P&C domain immediately becomes responsible for supporting the organization with the transformation. As enterprise agility is either a successor or a joint initiative with organizational agility, the initiatives need to be aligned. Some of these initiatives can be named as changing the organizational design toward squads, removing hierarchy in the organization, defining new roles and assigning the right people to those roles are a definite prerequisite, as explained in the organizational agility chapter. Considering all these tactical changes, the P&C departments should allocate enough resources to be able to respond to the requirements. On top, these dedicated resources should be trained with the new mindset, since a selection process of the product owner should not be approached as a typical project manager recruitment. In order to prepare the rest of the organization for what is approaching, the P&C teams should become a change agent prior to the transformation kick off.

It is then predictable that the role of P&C will not end with enabling the change of the structure. After the initial set up of tribes, squads and onboarding the product owners, scrum master etc., the domain should immediately, if possible even before the structure setup, concentrate on P&C processes and reshape them. The magnitude of change is much higher than any previous sort of transformation. So it would be beneficial to focus on those areas per process.

4.2.1.1 Recruitment

Let's start with a less controversial one, the change of recruitment process, which covers both internal assignment and external search and placement. The basic and well-known flow includes the hiring manager as an active decision-maker in the process. In hierarchical organizations, the hiring manager as the sole evaluator leads to lesser and/or slower adaptation of the joiners to the team culture. Also, the hiring manager in traditional organizations prioritizes the functional expertise rather than the mindset and behaviors. Related to that, the role the P&C teams play is mostly an operational contribution rather than designing the building blocks to the new collaborative company culture.

■ **Criteria:** The first sub-process is the selection criteria; where a new set of measures need to be designed in order to select the candidate with the highest adoption potential to the new ways of working, as well as the expertise.

If there is a lack of potential fit to the new mindset; a pricing specialist candidate with perfect analytical score on a pricing tool or an excellent software developer being eliminated in the selection process.

This is rather tough to be accepted at first by the recruiting leaders since they are used to pick the candidate with the best expertise, regardless of the rest. Many companies apply behavioral tests already, especially to the leadership levels; however, the leaders used to give little importance to the how part and underestimate those reports. This happens to such an extent that I have experienced a board member, pushing the P&C team to recruit a director, who was expected to lead a team of over 50 people, with a 10% score out of 100 in the leadership assessment.

So the P&C teams during this transition have to safeguard the culture and push for recruiting the right capabilities and mindset. Although new ways of working come together with a wide list of capabilities, collaborative, innovative, growth oriented and responsive features may be the ones to go for in the first place.

■ **Interviews:** As the hierarchy is removed and there is no single "manager", the selection process becomes a shared responsibility. Most commonly, this task is performed by collective evaluation of tribe leader, product owner and chapter leader, where they grade the candidate according to a predefined set of criteria, then share and evaluate.

In companies with higher maturity of agility, the team interviews the candidate and the decision is given by the peers. The direct report, who is generally the chapter lead, only has a social introduction to confirm the candidate. With peer recruiting, the team benefits from hiring the candidate that is best fit for the relevant team dynamics and the joiner adapts to the company easier.

■ **Assessments:** During the first year of transformation, it would be wise to leverage external sources for the assessments, especially for the new roles such as product owner or chapter lead, since there will be lack of know-how on the correct assessment criteria. Contracting an independent scrum master or an agile coach may ease the process. Once the key change agents are assigned to their roles, they might be the ones to take over the internal assessment activities.

Benefits: The process allows team members select their teammates themselves, so they take on the responsibility to pick the best candidates. The candidate combining the optimal level of technical expertise plus the right mindset is selected. The new joiners recruited with the help of their peers adapt to the company better and faster and have better engagement.

In addition, the selection of the right talent is a crucial step in terms of defining what the new company culture would be. Culture is a tough concept since it is extremely hard to change and one of the critical instruments to construct the new culture is to recruit the right people. Those newcomers will not just add themselves as plus one but also act as role models, who hopefully influence the others.

The P&C recruitment team, automatizing their operational tasks and rather concentrating on adding the right talents with the right mindset takes a more strategic position.

4.2.1.2 Performance Management

Whenever I am invited to a panel or conference to talk about agility, with no exceptions, performance management is the question I get asked the most. This is related to the strong link of performance evaluation with hierarchy. Due to the strong bond, the methods proposed may seem very unusual at first and harder to process so I need to add that they are applied to all different sorts of teams over the last years and brought positive value.

- **Feedback:** In traditional performance management, the feedback discussion takes place between the manager and the employee. Through the calendar year, these two parties frequently get together somehow but the topic of discussion is always the work, and there is hardly any feedback sharing or coaching. At the very end of the year, due to the premium salary distribution timeline, the conversation about performance takes place. In such an environment, only the work outputs, in order of the terms the "what" is evaluated by the manager.

  Whereas in agile organizations, the evaluation of the progress is continuous through the year and is performed by the teams. This is provided by the previously explained retrospective ceremonies. The team has a chance to evaluate each other's contributions in an hour-long retrospective by the end of each sprint, so in a biweekly manner. The scrum master is the facilitator of this ceremony, who brings different tools and methods to enable members to talk about each other. With the help of these retrospective sessions, the team members have a good understanding of their individual performance and their contribution to their team.

- **Evaluation:** The evaluation stage includes the one-to-one discussion of the score, which used to be only about the employee's outputs rather than how the team as a whole performed or whether the business even succeeded. In addition, since this is a once-a-year activity, the manager has hardly the wholesome view of the employee with minor feedback received from the people the employee works with. So it is safe to assume that only the general perception of the employee is leveraged by the line manager.

  In the agile evaluation process, there is a collective effort to assess the member from all points of view. The collective notion comes from inclusion of all members of the team that contribute to the effort.

  To specify this, I detail two different approaches depending on the maturity of agility in the organization, via illustrated examples: Assume a tribe with four squads and three chapters, where "Member X" is part of Squad 2 and belongs to the B chapter (Figure 4.2).

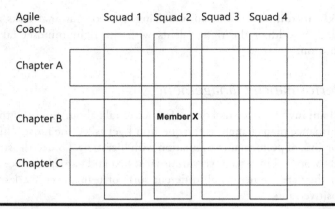

Figure 4.2   Tribe member belonging to a chapter and a squad.

- **The agile leadership evaluation:** In this model, the opinion leaders of the new working model, the product owner, the chapter lead and the agile coach are the evaluators. Each member is evaluated by all members of this committee. However, Member X is primarily commented by the CL B, the second squad's PO and agile coach as a default commenter. If there are other members who have observed or directly experienced either positive or negative qualities, they also comment when Member X is being discussed. In this way, each member of the tribe is commonly evaluated. After the end of each performance cycle, Member X is notified with the commentaries with full transparency by their CLs (Figure 4.3).
- **Cross-teams' evaluation:** The second model is rather ambitious but serves the agile philosophy completely. It is about replacing individual contribution with team contribution and removing all layers of evaluation where the members of the teams are present during discussion.

    First of all, each squad evaluates themselves as a team by looking at the whole year discussions about their performance based on the performed

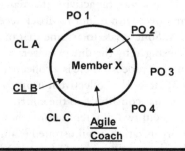

Figure 4.3   Within squad evaluation.

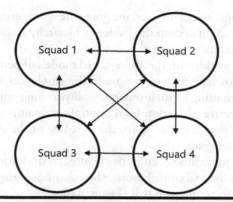

Figure 4.4 Evaluation among teams.

retrospectives. They align on a common perspective and form a narrative on what they have achieved, and how they did it. The narrative should include the outcomes the team created, the business that they have developed, and also how they worked together, whether they have experimented or innovated together. After each squad completes this preparation, all teams gather in a panel where a representative from each squad, not necessarily the product owner, explains their achievements to each other (Figure 4.4).

After the pitches are over each member of the squad evaluates the other squads by grading their performance. Their final grades are announced by P&C and after learning the scores related to their evaluation, the squad meets again, separately, to review the comments and the evaluations they have received and have a year-end final retrospective (Figure 4.5).

■ **Calibration**: If we were to conduct a survey of employees around the world about the corporate term they are irritated the most, my guess is that it would be "calibration". It symbolizes the gap between what the employer believes and

Evaluating Squad	BUSINESS OUTCOME	EXPERIMENTING	INNOVATION	COLLABORATION
B Squad	4	2	3	5
C Squad	....	....	....	....
D Squad	....	....	....	....

A Squad

Overall Squad Score: 3

Figure 4.5 Overall squad performance evaluation.

how the manager sees. However, the grade the managers assume to give to the employee gets calibrated up the ladder or hierarchy until the board members compare and adjust the grades.

In the new world, with the above-stated models of performance evaluation, this term is not replaced but removed. The employees know what and how they are contributing to their outcomes all year long with constant feedback and get a collective evaluation from multiple evaluators. Also considering the ladders of the pyramid don't exist, the outcome of the evaluation is equal to the performance grade.

In the second method of collective grading, if the leadership team wishes to identify the individual contributors, who contribute below or above the team, there is a way to accomplish that (Figure 4.6).

When this personal differentiation method is preferred, at the calibration stage, which means after the squad is notified of their group score, the squad members vote for others, whether they are below or above the squad's average contribution. In this example, the Squad A concludes the cross-squad evaluation with an average score of three. Then the four members of the squad fill an evaluation for the other three member's contribution in case it is different from the team performance. In this example, three votes were given to member 1 as the above contributor, and three votes were given to member 4 as below-average contribution.

This way both the team performance is evaluated collectively by their peers as well as allowing outlier individual contribution to be discovered. So the always favored individual competition among the members of the teams does not have to disappear. However, the main importance is given to the team's position, so squads in a way compete with each other to get the best grade.

I am aware that the new approach to performance management is demolishing the longest-lived concept of classical performance evaluation; however, this doesn't mean employees are not giving their best.

Benefits: Obviously the main benefit is that the team collectively owns the success and performs to be able to achieve whatever is needed. Boundaries and job

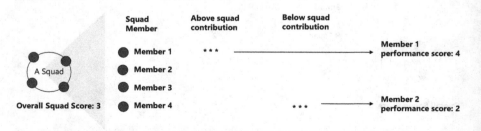

Figure 4.6   Squad member evaluation based on squad performance.

descriptions no longer act as drawbacks. I should also note that bringing the team as the main focus is helping to concentrate on what the collective ambition was and whether it was met. What I mean is when the business targets are fragmented among different boxes around the company, the individual seeks an award for their portion of the work, where the holistic picture cannot be evaluated.

Case: I was a part of a team where we launched a new business product with five members of five different functions. The product was generating revenue, 1,000-unit sales in the first year; however, it was 25% of what we had anticipated. At the end of the year, when it was performance evaluation time with respective managers, all five of us were evaluated based on our individual contributions to the product development, and every member of the team received good marks. If I looked one by one it wasn't wrong; the system was working perfectly so the developer did the job sufficiently, there was customer interaction so the customer excellence specialist's approach was on track, the customer surveys were coming positively so the after-sales services were well delivered. However, overall the project didn't hit the target.

So when the collective outcome is evaluated rather than individual contribution, in my example, the product team would have been graded according to the success of the product, which was 25%. Furthermore, when our team were then targeted collectively for the business outcome, first of all we would have projected the revenue more realistically, for instance, 1,500 in sales rather than the 4,000 forecast, and then would go beyond our job descriptions or areas of expertise, to get the 1,000 sales to the 1,500 ambition.

There is another benefit dimension which is related to employee reaction since the link between employee's expectation and manager's perception is broken. There is no longer demotivation of employees caused by the classic "your work is not visible enough" escape way. The performance is linked to what the team produces, and every member is responsible for doing their best even beyond their job descriptions.

4.2.1.3 Career Architecture

Leaving the most complex topic to last; career architecture is changing drastically with agility. This process includes the P&C department's management of the job grade levels in relation to the organizational design, or shortly promotion or career ladder process as commonly used. Currently, career ladder management is a concept that is largely similar among companies. This claim is due to the fact that there are top two to three global HR consultancy companies that provide job-level evaluation services to majority of global corporates and large-scale local companies. So these HR consultancy companies are in fact acting as an aggregator that streamlines the process all over the world. Consider a business analyst in the FMCG sector located in France and deciding to move to Spain to work for a bank, the grade is convertible to the destination and it is possible for the analyst to know what level of career move this corresponds to.

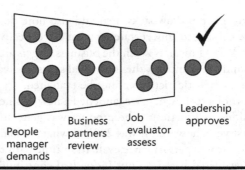

People
manager
demands

Business
partners
review

Job
evaluator
assess

Leadership
approves

Figure 4.7   Career management funnel.

The career management flow is simply around the annual P&C cycle, usually at the end of the calendar year, where the P&C business partners collect the candidates for promotion and evaluate the relevant positions with the job evaluating consultancy companies. The positions which have been verified as promotion goes through departmental selection and finally in companywide calibration. As illustrated above, all these steps underline a heavy elimination that only a lucky few are approved for a career move (Figure 4.7).

The issues that rise with this flow is; first as in performance management there is a calibration involved and the decision is based on the view of the people manager. Each calibration step along the way, the direct manager's voice is less heard. Imagine an organization not as simple as this but the people manager who is demanding the grade increase have three layers before the board level where the final calibration is made. The employee, who first of all has to make the direct manager believe in her contribution and make her list appear in the "list of demands", has almost seven levels of other barriers to be able to receive that promotion. It is not easy for the direct manager as well, trying to persuade the above layers of managers that this employee should get the promotion. Within my role in P&C, I have seen so many talents fade away due to this system; either staying with the company but slowly drawing away or trying their chance in a different company.

Another issue is the box bounded promotion, which means an employer's grade is limited by the direct manager's grade and can only increase if the manager leaves the position. This limitation is caused by the vertical structure of the organization, tying the management to the direct reports.

Case: To clarify this situation, assume a retail company where a grade 4 Product Manager, who has a grade 4 peer Campaign Manager reporting to a grade 5 Marketing Director. The Product Manager is a talented leader with great potential and has a risk of attrition with offers from a competitor company. In traditional organizations, there is no solution for this bottleneck other than offering the talent another grade position (if any open positions exist); however, the role is not compatible with the employee's background or career interests (Figure 4.8).

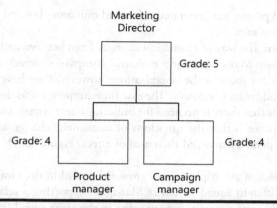

Figure 4.8 A case of marketing function career management.

In agile career architecture, the notion of box bounded career management is removed and replaced by a position in the matrix structure as illustrated below. The Product Manager in the previous example becomes a member of a related tribe and can grow as long as she takes additional responsibilities from the area provided to the tribe. These additional responsibilities can be either vertical, which means other tasks within the squad or horizontal, which refers to expanding her services within the marketing chapter but this time beyond the squad. In rare cases, she can even stretch herself toward an outside tribe duty as well. The decision of this expansion should be a mutual agreement between the related departments that her skills and/ or expertise would be an applicant in that team (Figure 4.9).

■ **Application:** This way, the career moves do not happen through the year (since there are no assignments to any empty boxes) but rather at the end of each year, the P&C business partners collect candidates for individual growth from leaders in the organization. The case includes real-world evidence of how

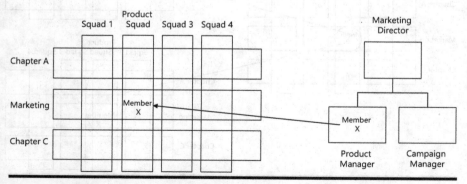

Figure 4.9 Agile career management structure.

the related person has generated value and outcomes beyond his/her previous contribution area.

■ **Evaluation:** The way of evaluation changes from box evaluation to individual contribution. Many of the job evaluator companies already have this sort of assessment for roles in the organization; however, they have been used only for low-grade roles previously. The ease for enterprises who decide to apply the approach is that there is no need for building a new system for evaluation. The only difference is that the questions of assessment change according to how much the person expanded their area of effect (Figure 4.10).

The area of impact of an employee can grow either within the same expertise, contributing to a different squad (Product Manager supporting a relaunch activity in 3rd squad) or different expertise contributing in the same squad (Product Manager in the Product Squad takes over to business analysis which belongs to chapter A). In some cases, contributing beyond the business initiatives are observed (e.g. sustainability, innovation)

■ **Approval:** The approval process which used to be performed similarly to performance rating calibration is replaced with a simple approval. The limiting criteria become the compensation and benefits package limitation. The leaders approve the candidate who meets the grade assessment and are prioritized within the compensation budget to receive their promotion.

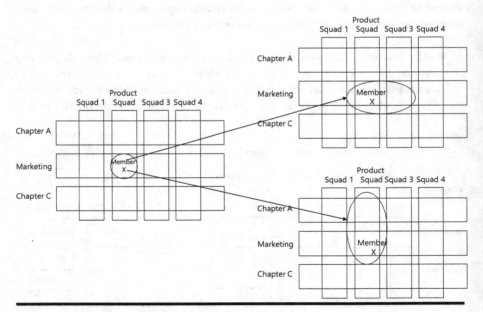

Figure 4.10 Individual contribution career evaluation.

In some cases, the top management may add a general review session to candidates above a certain threshold (for top percentile grade owners) to ensure cross evaluation of the candidate and to make sure there is a general positive view. This means, if the grades in that company range from three to ten, three being the entry position and 10 being the grade of the General Manager, the company may choose to evaluate the candidates moving above grade 7, to be reviewed at the board collectively. This way each leader confirms the move with respect to the corporate culture, although they may not directly with the promoting candidate.

Benefits: This model of career architecture has many benefits, but among all is allowing a space for growth mindset. HBR explains growth mindset terminology as individuals, who believe their talents can be developed [31]. In a traditional organization where the boxes limit employees to functional job descriptions, one can't find the nourishing environment to explore new horizons. As a result, it became a custom to act within the boundaries of the given job descriptions. There are cases where volunteer employees take some additional responsibilities informally and help other teams; however, those kinds of behaviors cannot be awarded as a career step in the traditional career management approach.

Whereas in the agile career architecture model, the same person with the growth mindset has the ability to create value in different business areas and get acknowledgment for her actions. This conversion is called shifting from T-shaped mindset [32]. T-shaped employee is what we see in all organizations at all levels, an employee with an expertise in a topic (the vertical of T) and general information about the company (the horizontal of T) (Figure 4.11).

The more the employee works on the topic, the depth of expertise increases: For instance, an accounting specialist in the Finance department, may perform this role for even 20 years. Through these years, the employee's expertise in accounting

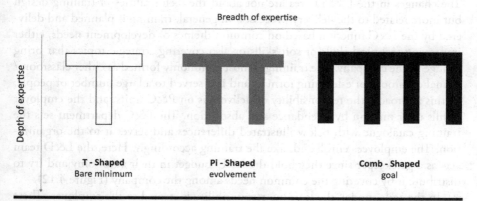

Figure 4.11   T, Pi and Comb shaped profiles.

increases and may reach an optimal level in the first five years. So the additional value of remaining 15 years gradually declines. However, if there is a growth environment for him and he is able to take on additional duties from the financial planning team, the person is becoming a Pi shaped expert. Later in his career, he can develop himself beyond the borders of the finance function and become comb shaped.

This leads to a true win-win situation for the employer as well as the employee. The employee benefits from becoming comb-shaped since he has more career opportunities, he doesn't have to repeat the work in accounting when he is well experienced in procurement as well. He can grow the career ladder and there is no grade ceiling for his position, which means his salary base can increase so there is a direct link to employee's financial benefit.

In my personal career experience, being a generalist and having the comb-shaped expertise helped me not only with my promotional moves but also to gain flexibility in career switches. Since today's corporate environment is not stable, company structures can continuously change. Through 15+ years of professional career, I experienced the company I work for having a merger, or a complete shutdown of business or moving to another location which all forced me to take another position within or outside that company. So from an employee perspective, the VUCA environment applies to the career planning as well.

Similar to the employee, the employer realizes certain benefits: talent retention and attraction. The member of the team who is highly talented and on top willing to contribute more to the team's success has an ability to perform and outgrow himself, as well as the team he belongs to. In addition to that the leaders have flexibility to manage temporary shortfalls better, in cases when more than one employee takes a leave in a team or when there is unexpected work in a certain unit and help is needed.

4.2.1.4 Learning & Development

The changes in the L & D area are not about the technicalities of training design but more related to the delivery processes. In general, training is planned and delivered by the P&C function based on common themes of development needs, either improving technical skills or soft skills or also covering strategic topics that bring change to the company. The training is most commonly formed as either classroom/virtual classroom or e-learning formats and it is served to a large number of people. In this approach, the responsibility of delivery is on P&C units, and the employer fulfills their mission by attendance and absorption. The P&C department sets the training catalogue with below illustrated differences and serves it to the organization. The employees enroll and take the training accordingly. Here, the L&D team acts as a gatekeeper since they hold the L&D budget in their autonomy and try to distribute it by covering the common needs among the company (Figure 4.12).

In the agile model, the learning responsibility is steered to the employee. There is no generic list of training where the P&C units hold the budget and decide on the

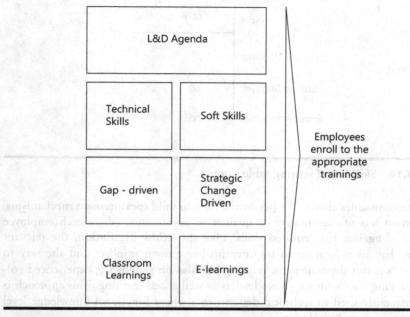

Figure 4.12   L&D catalogue.

distribution. There is instead a catalogue of ideal learning materials defined for each role and expertise area. This time they are not pushed toward as compulsory steps for performing the task (apart from legal and compliance modules where the employees have to complete and get certified), and it becomes the employee's main responsibility to make sure they have each skill developed in order to perform that task.

Companies can provide a comprehensive role – capability matrix as illustrated below, where the required hard and soft skills are plotted against the new roles. Each person holding one of the new roles can find his/her status regarding the skills and the types of learnings and create a learning plan to develop themselves (Figure 4.13).

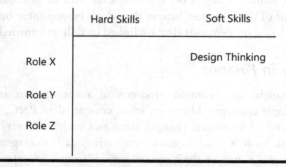

Figure 4.13   Role-based hard and soft skill development matrix.

Role X	Score
Design Thinking:	75
Growth Mindset:	60
Entrepreneurship:	80

Figure 4.14 Skill-based scoring table sample.

Some companies also tie the personal efforts to solid measurement mechanisms, with certain sets of quantitative or qualitative assessments, where each employee is evaluated against the required skills. Like the below illustration, the relevant employee has an obligation to improve his/her growth mindset and the way to achieve this is not dependent on training but also on shadowing experienced colleagues, asking for mentoring from leaders as well as self-learning. This approach is more frequently used in technical departments where functional knowledge level defines the work quality (Figure 4.14).

Benefits: With the changing approach of L&D which has long been pushed as a service from P&C toward a pull culture, the companies will benefit from more engaging employees in their learning journeys since they have the full responsibility.

A major shift in thinking I have observed when L&D offerings change is that the employee feels they cannot rely on some expert in the L&D department, who will anyway find and offer some important learnings. They rather feel they are in the driver's seat and sense an obligation to find the most needed development areas and ask for coaching from their leaders on feedback related to how much they have progressed within those areas.

Another benefit is better management of the L&D budget where there are no mass trainings where employees leave by complaining how much time they have lost. The budget is not managed on a macro level with mass classroom training where at least half of the attendees believe they don't belong there but rather spent on a micro level based on demands that are linked to skill or knowledge gaps.

4.2.2 Agility in Finance

Finance and financial management processes of a corporation are also highly affected by the agile concepts. However, when compared to P&C, there is a difference in the level of structural changes since not each and every sub-function is directly altered. So it is wiser to spare accounting, cash management and procurement which will continue their operations with small adjustments. Whereas financial planning and control, cost management and investment management areas are directly affected. Similar to the P&C topics like performance management and career architecture, the financial process changes are also quite different than usual. However, with an open-minded analysis and help of the cases I cover, it is possible to envision the impact.

4.2.2.1 Financial Planning

In the financial planning cycle, companies try to estimate and plan from where they stand today in terms of their profit and loss structures, organization structure and headcounts, channels and distribution dynamics, market share against competition toward what they are planning to achieve in upcoming years. In a way, it is an estimation of what the whole business structure will be like in each consecutive year from today onward. The annual planning is usually kicked off during summer and gets busier through the fall and submitted toward the end of the year. So it is safe to claim that the process from beginning to end takes around six months of employees responsible for providing input to the estimates (Figure 4.15).

The issue of the cycle, apart from the time-consuming process, is the lack of link between the plans and reality. As illustrated in the below graphic, it is widely experienced that the actual revenue generated in corporations stays repetitively low when compared to plans. This chart is driven by my previous experience; however, many companies can derive the same results with a retrospective analysis. The reason behind the lack of correlation is that the planning works as a top-down target and marks the position that the head office would like to achieve. So the head office always asks for a stretch (sometimes even impossible) target rather than an achievable one (Figure 4.16).

In the agile model, there is no top-down commitment of long-term planning. So there are no set targets that are pushed toward the teams with hierarchy.

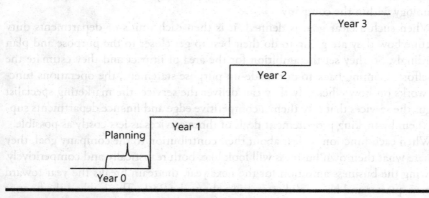

Figure 4.15   3-year financial planning cycle.

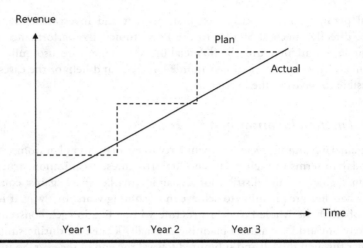

Figure 4.16 Actual vs plan comparison of long term financial planning.

The management is instead responsible for clearly communicating the common purpose that the company is aligned on. The purpose definition should not be similar to the vision and mission statements that companies used to (and some still do) print their walls at the top of the reception desk.

The purpose statement is the common goal that each and every employee agrees on and it defines why they are coming to work each day. It should be ambitious and uniting. The purpose statement should clearly draw the path and include the ambitious goal they want to reach. It can be "to be the most preferred, best service providing company with the lowest cost" in their area, which can call attention to customer orientation that they are aiming as well as the competitive positioning of their area of work so that financial revenue can be derived from there and on top highlight the cost of service ambition which can be provided with higher use of technology within the company.

When such a clear goal is defined, it is then each unit's or departments duty to define how they are going to do their best to get closer to the purpose and plan accordingly. So they set the ambition for the area of impact and they estimate the best effort. Coming back to our made-up purpose statement, the operations function works on how efficiently they can deliver the service, the marketing specialist designs the services that give them a competitive edge and finance departments support them by making procurement deals of those services as less costly as possible.

When each function is clear about their contribution to the company goal, they estimate what their own business will look like, both realistically and competitively. Knowing the business ambition for the next year, the team breaks the year toward the next quarter and has a solid estimation about the P&L. This is when the finance business partners get heavily involved and gather the latest estimate of the following 90-day period (Figure 4.17).

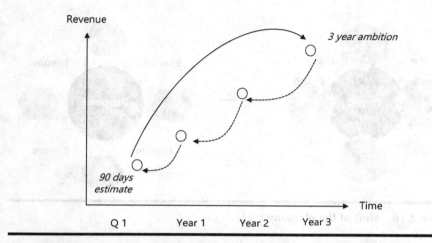

Figure 4.17   Backcasting method applied instead of three year planning.

As the above chart illustrates, the purpose statement that refers to the end of three years declares an ambition. In our example, it was to become the most preferred service providing company, so the revenue ambition is about having the largest market share in the market. Similarly, the cost chart would be looking like this on the reverse, setting a three-year ambition cost, gradually decreasing so that the company becomes the lowest cost service company. After the long-term ambition is numerically set, the rest is to define where the company should be by the end of each year, so that the three-year goal would be achievable. This is named as the midterm outcome which is numerically defined as well, and the only real planning is done for the next 90 days, to state what would be the revenue generated in the next quarter.

The methodology in estimating the future and planning today is called backcasting. The term is explained by Holmberg and Robert as, planning under uncertain circumstances. It is a method in which future desired conditions are envisioned and steps are defined to attain those conditions [33]. The method was designed by Robinson in 1990 to define how to manage ambiguous environments [34]. However, when we consider our current business environment, there are less known than unknowns. So it is rather surprising that only a small minority of corporations adapt their planning cycles.

Benefits: There are two different types of benefits: first, the efficiency driven from the removal of lengthy planning processes, and second, the flexibility of the near future estimation on how we manage the business (Figure 4.18).

The first point is related to how time and effort consuming the planning cycle used to be. The below chart demonstrates the reformation well. The left-hand side circle is the standard annual planning cycle where almost six months of a calendar year was consumed with extensive effort of planning, which left the rest of it actually executing. This might seem surprising at first, thinking it is the financial team's

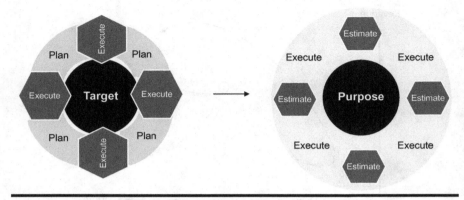

Figure 4.18 Shift of the planning cycle.

dedication, but unfortunately the financial planners need members from all business units in order to run their cycles. Comparatively on the right-hand side, the focus shifts from planning to execution substantially. With the common purpose in mind, the teams estimate their close future and concentrate the rest on trying to achieve their ambition.

The second topic was about the ambiguity in planning forward. I accept that there were times when estimating the evolution of a business was in fact possible, back then, if you were taking into account the right financial variables, observing the competitor strategies, listening to the customer thoughts via surveys, you were able to predict what the figures will be. However, year over year, as the effect of VUCA becomes more significant in our environments, the possibility of correct prediction diminishes.

To clarify the point, just imagine a planner of a finance department, in a brick-and-mortar business, working on 2020 shop distribution strategy back in 2019, of course with no idea of an upcoming pandemic where all bricks-and-mortar business will spend at least half of the year shut down. However, even in not such drastic changes, when there is a target and the business is suffering from an external condition, companies do not accept failure and pivot fast enough.

4.2.2.2 Budget Management

After the planning cycle is completed, the head office allocates a predefined budget to the affiliate or if it's a local conglomerate, the center allocates the budget. The amount of the budget is configured by the revenue commitments and growth potentials of each operating unit. Then the finance business partners have the responsibility to clearly define the category budgets, allocated to the use of the cost center departments. The common cost centers generic to all sectors are Human Resources,

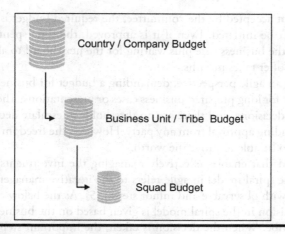

Figure 4.19   Allocation of the country budget.

Information Technologies and Marketing. Of course, the magnitude may vary according to the sector, for instance, IT costs of an e-commerce company may overshoot people costs (Figure 4.19).

After the departmental budgets are set, the next action is to divide and segment it in a deeper level to units. An example of budget segmentation for IT would be the division of hardware, software, network, outsourced services and maintenance.

When the subcategory allocation of cost centers is completed, it is critical through the financial calendar to abide by the plan and manage expenditures accordingly in order to ensure that the budget holders act as a gate through the year, for upcoming demands.

The gatekeeping can be performed simply as assigning an approver for usual expenses or running a committee structure where certain leaders review the proposal and appraise the expenditure. So corporations make sure the departments stay within budget and spend the budget effectively. There are mainly two types of budget approval: the first is the escalated approval, which is given by the direct line and applies operational costs like employee travel or meal expenses, or purchasing orders where the approver is selected based on the amount or the type of expense.

The second type is committee approvals, where the department seeking approval has to present the case to the related committee. Members of these committees are defined by the work procedures and are generally represented by executive board level. A common example is the portfolio management committee where the Vice Presidents of IT, Finance, Marketing and Sales get together to evaluate the project initiation requests from all departments. The projects are related to business development ideas, new product or system change offers. In order to present the case, the approval seeker team prepares a business case, justifying the amount demanded.

If the idea is not accepted by the committee, the required budget is not granted so the project can't be initiated. Even if it is approved, the time spent with both the preparation of the business case plus waiting for the next board to allocate the time to listen to the offer takes months.

Whereas in an agile perspective, demanding a budget for business-critical items should not wait for long prepared business cases or presentations. The team is autonomous to take decisions, and there are no thresholds to escalate decisions. They do not ask for spending approval from any party. However, the freedom comes with the responsibility to be able to prove the worth.

The method that enables effectively managing the investments is called spiral investment. The spiral model in agile refers to the iterative management of a large-scale initiative with observable and minor steps [35]. As the below chart shows, the investment decision in the spiral model is given based on the business plan requirement, by the tribe. When the decision is taken, the important step is to break the spending plan in relation to the key milestones or epics planned to be delivered along the project's timeline. Those epics are configured and plotted on the investment chart as levels 1, 2 and 3, and there is a relative spending release corresponding to these levels. The release does not take place until the first epic is completed, the results of the release are evaluated and the outcomes are found justifying further investment (Figure 4.20).

Case: To better clarify the concept we can assume a business unit deciding to implement a comprehensive customer platform with integrated website, social media pages, and a mobile application. The team invites some vendors and asks for calculation of the cost of building such a platform and the best offer they receive is 5m $. Since this is a very significant investment, the team works on fragmenting the offer to separable releases, where they can test the customer reactions and decide on

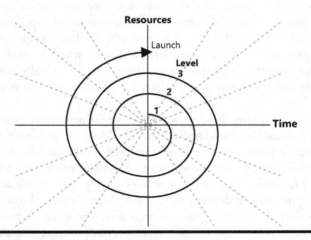

Figure 4.20   Spiral investment method.

the next steps. They define the levels of separation as three and name the first release as social media, then a web page and finally a mobile application. The reason for the selection of this order is due to increasing complexity from the first level, respectively, toward two and three. In cost terms, this also means the cost of the initial package will be less than the other two. Later the vendor company is called back and asked to resubmit their development effort as independent contracts for these three demands and offer pricing for each delivery. The company resubmits three separate offers this time, 0.5m $ for release one, 1.5m $ for release two and 3m $ for the last. This way, the company still may choose to spend the whole 5m $ on the new customer platform; however, this time they have the chance to observe the customer penetration ratio and decide on the next steps if value is realized.

In this case, the team parks the ideas and excitement about all different platforms and starts with the social media campaign, traces the customer reaction to the generated service and either confirms the hypothesis and goes to the second step of investment or pivots the idea to a different approach. These steps and tracking data are transparently shared so can be reviewed when necessary.

Benefits: Like the planning cycle, removal of the demand management processes allows significant efficiency, when the time spent for preparation for the committees, including assumptions, project plans, business cases and ROIs etc. is considered. This allows a shorter time to market the output.

When I was responsible for a cost center department, I came up with an initiative that was going to have a significant cost reduction effect and only required a minor system development. It was requesting 50K $ to generate at least 1m $ saving in the first year. The portfolio manager of the company asked me to present the proposition to the Portfolio Committee. I gladly accepted, however, learned that the next one was going to be held in three months; it didn't affect my excitement about the project since I thought I could use the time to prepare for my presentation. I thought it would be just preparing a 1–2 slide executive summary about the idea, however, was warned by the portfolio manager that I have to provide a full business case, which included financial estimation of every possible scenario. In order to get the file ready, I had to steal time of three other departments during these months. Later the portfolio manager called me saying that the committee agenda was full of other propositions and mine can only be presented in six months! With the "gained" time, my manager advised me that an executive summary wouldn't look well prepared enough so suggested a whole deck, so the slides went up to 30. After all, I presented a long deck together with an overly detailed business case, within the three minutes given to me (I originally had 20 minutes but was asked to squeeze my presentation since the board was tired), after six months of waiting. All for accepting to pay 50K $ for a first-year 1m $ gain. The CFO replied "of course" after seeing the solid ROI in the first minute, but they still granted me two minutes to present the executive summary.

The second critical benefit is that in the traditional way when a budget is allocated to a project, it is commonly not tracked in respect to the initial business case that is presented in the portfolio committee. So the promised outcomes are not evaluated retrospectively. If a project fails in its Key Performance Indicators (KPIs) or overspends, there is less room for corrective actions.

Coming back to the board room example, waiting along with so many project initiatives, knowing how much all colleagues prepared for their approval, none were asked back whether the committed values were ever generated. Whereas in the spiral model, each step of the program is made with proving benefits of the previous. Like the customer platform case above, if the social media release fails to deliver the assumed revenue, the project team is expected to terminate the second and third releases to not create any further loss of money. So it is ironically less risky to walk away from the demand planning process.

4.2.2.3 Financial Control

The third step of the financial management cycle is highly linked to the changing dynamics in the initial two since this step represents controlling the initial financial plan in accordance with the demand management actions through the year.

Financial control is the set of procedures that ensure the financial use of resources are in line with company procedures and plans [36]. The overall profitability management of a company is controlled by the finance department and as a second line, by an independent financial auditor. Since the process is the core of tracking the overall performance of the company, it is closely monitored by all top management.

Due to the criticality of the process, a tracking mechanism called KPIs is used as the means to ensure that the business dynamics are going according to the annual plan.

The KPIs have certain characteristics which define how the control process is shaped. First of all, they are linked to performance targets so are top down. They are given to the teams at the beginning of the financial year, and the performance of the unit depends on how well they perform in accordance with the measurement criteria. In addition, they are fixed for usually a three-year period and since they are handled rigidly, the market dynamics within those three years do not affect the targets. Finally in terms of controlling process, the identification of issues regarding the performance is done retrospectively.

In the agile way of financial management, even the term "controlling" changes into "tracking" and the financial controller role becomes financial business partners. The names of courses are not critical; however, they carry a message remarking the shift of structure from retrospective analysis and enforcement of consequences, toward the finance becoming a partner who follows the way business performs and supports them by tracking related data throughout the year.

In order to shift this process, the long served KPIs were required to be replaced as well, which brought the objectives and key results (OKRs). Niven and Lamonte [37] define the OKRs as a thinking framework that seeks to ensure employees work together, to focus on their efforts to make measurable contributions to take their company forward [37]. The OKRs enable the direct link between our goals and the

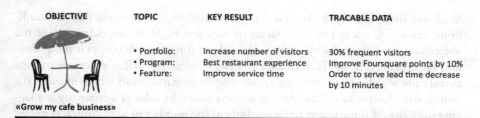

OBJECTIVE	TOPIC	KEY RESULT	TRACABLE DATA
	• Portfolio:	Increase number of visitors	30% frequent visitors
	• Program:	Best restaurant experience	Improve Foursquare points by 10%
	• Feature:	Improve service time	Order to serve lead time decrease by 10 minutes
«Grow my cafe business»			

Figure 4.21   An example of OKR.

outcomes to be realized in order to achieve them. A team that is tracking their OKRs constantly have the ability to understand whether they are on track with respect to their long-term ambitions. They also serve as warning signs, to reflect problematic areas that need further concentration (Figure 4.21).

Since the OKRs can also be leveraged in our daily lives, I would like to give a non-corporate example this time. Unlike other business cases, assume you own a seaside café in a popular summer resort. If growing your café business revenue is your ambition, you know that you need to increase the number of visitors. If you have a tool to track the number of customers and detect the loyal ones who are frequently eating at your cafe, you can ensure a certain revenue. While you concentrate on customer flow, you should also keep a track of the experience and service level simultaneously. Being able to trace these outcomes enables you to manage your business in real terms. The same applies to business unit management in corporations (Figure 4.22).

When compared to KPIs, the OKRs are not top down delivered, but rather the team defines their objectives in accordance to the company vision. They are not

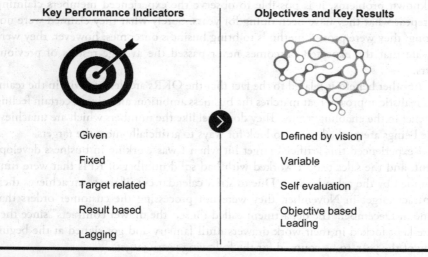

Key Performance Indicators	Objectives and Key Results
Given	Defined by vision
Fixed	Variable
Target related	Self evaluation
Result based	Objective based Leading
Lagging	

Figure 4.22   KPIs vs OKRs.

fixed and rigid, like the KPIs, and can be adapted to the changing market conditions, crisis, and entries to the market or regulations. Since the definition of the objective is the responsibility of the team and not forced top down, so is the evaluation (as explained in the Performance Management section). The success is tracked as real time with leading indicators rather than lagging indicators which measure the results. An example to differentiate two terms would be sales of a company is a lagging indicator, it is measured retrospectively as the number of sales contracts signed through the given period. A company can only use lagging indicators as a post-event evaluation whereas leading indicators are the critical data showing whether the company is taking the right actions to enable sales, for instance, the number of proposals submitted to the customer in a consultancy company is indicating whether there would be any sales revenue generated.

Benefits: With all the comparisons explained above, it is clear that although leaving the KPIs behind might generate concerns regarding control, the OKRs on the contrary enable a more realistic and sensible tracking mechanism. It allows realizing the risks of achieving the desired results in early stages and enables you to adapt your backlog with an alternative direction. It also allows not to be persistent to the given targets which leads to missing the blind spots of either risks or opportunities.

To enable this, I always offer teams to make use of the OKRs, not only for reporting purposes but also as a tool that enables data-driven decision-making. Experience in an area is certainly highly valuable to offer solutions and suggestions to make the work better. If overused, this power can also easily turn into a blinder, when the decisions on next actions are solely given according to previous experience. When employees with high tenure start working on agility, I have frequently observed the planning sessions led by what is known and safe. Whereas sprint planning is the platform to generate new ideas, come up with innovative solutions to known problems, it is possible to observe the experienced members claiming to repeat what they have been doing for years. Surely what they claimed were not wrong, they were proven methods to bring business outcomes; however, they were so safe that the expected outcomes never passed the average results of previous years.

Another benefit is related to the fact that the OKRs are defined within the team, in a realistic approach that matches the business ambition, and gives a certain feeling of relief to the enabling teams. They don't feel like the numbers which are unachievable beings are pushed or try to look for ways to artificially meet the targets.

I experienced this artificial target hit when I was working in business development, and the sales team I worked with had solid number of KPIs that were time bounded by the calendar year. Due to strict calendar cut, if the team achieves their contract target in November, they were not processing the customer orders that came in December. The department called those, "the drawer contracts" since they were kept locked in their work drawers until January and got signed at the beginning of the year, to be counted for the following year's target.

4.2.3 Agility in Marketing

After analyzing the changes in two different support functions in the organization, Human Resources and Finance, it is a useful switch to a business function which is greatly affected by the agile principles. The support functions are reshaped by their sub-segments and their related processes, whereas marketing is shaken from its core, which means all related branches of work are adapting to the new philosophy. This core can be named as customer orientation. This may seem trivial since Strydom et al. define marketing as what customers want and need and directing the business resources to meet those needs [38]. However, in traditional marketing the company serves the customer with an expertise and revenue-driven approach, which translates into doing what the marketing department thinks what the customer needs and what would generate more sales. The higher the presence of the firm in the market, larger the customer serving experience accumulation, and as a consequence greater vocational blindness takes over. In this chapter, we explore newer approaches to customer experience management through the lenses of design thinking principles.

4.2.3.1 Insight-Driven Customer Proposition

Customer insight management is an approach that is often overlooked even in traditional marketing since it is commonly blocked by the experience bias. And when it is applied, market research methodology is often used to understand the customer reactions. A market research is the process of determining the value of a product or service which is provided by a company to its customer segment or potential customers [39]. So it is by nature an attempt to measure how the produced output serves the customer. If we attempt to reason backward, first the business idea turns into an output, and then customer reaction to the finished good is measured and assessed. As covered in the OKR section, this is a lagging measurement approach rather than leading, and the customer reaction is gathered too late (Figure 4.23).

With this approach, the business investment is rather a gamble, and the product remains in the market if it brings certain revenue, even if it doesn't match the initial proposition. Since the design, development and distribution costs are already invested and can be considered as sunk costs, even if the realized sales is 10% of the original business case, there is no business benefit of drawing the product out of the market (Figure 4.24).

| A new product / service idea is generated | ⇨ | The product / service is developed | ⇨ | The product / service is launched | ⇨ | Customers reaction is measured | ⇨ | Remains in the market if successful |

Figure 4.23 Traditional product development approach.

Design cost | Development cost | Delivery cost | Marketing cost | Total Cost of Product

Figure 4.24 Total cost of product development.

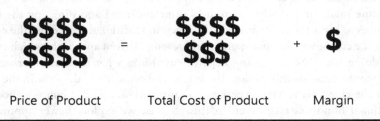

Price of Product | Total Cost of Product | Margin

Figure 4.25 Cost-based product pricing.

If the pricing methodology of the company is cost-based pricing (cost-based pricing is determining the price as a combination of all types of costs plus adding a sales margin), which is most common in large-sized corporations, then the price you will set for your product or service will even be overpriced since it includes all the sunk cost [40] (Figure 4.25).

In other words, the amount we price our products is a combination of the cost we build up and we fill all these functionalities, or key features to make the cost even go higher, without even knowing if the product itself is desired by a mass number of customers.

For instance, the Product Manager of kettles in an electronics retailer can come up with an innovative idea, to develop a kettle which has separate buttons for the type of drink you boil the water, like 70 degrees for coffee and 100 degrees for tea. The idea is certainly innovative; however, the company should first consider whether the cost of this new kettle will be purchasable before accepting all these additional costs of both design and development.

In an agile way, as quoted by Robert Half, "when the customer comes first, the customer will last": the order of the flow is reversed in order to hear the voice of the customer. But it is not just about the order since you put the insight gathering before the design, the question becomes "what do you need from our company?" instead of "what is your opinion of the service we are providing you?" (Figure 4.26).

This method is named as Design Thinking, which emerged in the 1980s in Palo Alto, California in the context of teaching engineers that there is a purpose of design, which is the customer and "what for" questions should always be asked first [41]. Design thinking is accepted as the initiation step of any agile development initiative since it is highly connected to insight and data-driven decision-making.

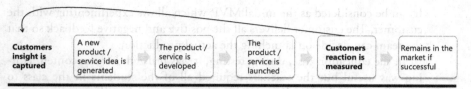

| Customers insight is captured | A new product / service idea is generated | The product / service is developed | The product / service is launched | Customers reaction is measured | Remains in the market if successful |

Figure 4.26 Customer insight driven product development process.

The basic principles of application of design thinking are building empathy with the customer, thinking like you are in their shoes, thinking out of the box to come up with innovative solutions and finally failing fast to make the investment for solutions that are worth.

The process of design thinking is allowing the above principles to work in perfect order.

Let's look into the process steps with an example:

■ Step 1 – Need finding: Exploring real customer issues, either explicit or implicit. The implicit needs are not known or voiced by the customers; however, they respond positively when those needs are met.

  During the initial month of the pandemic, all of a sudden the schools had to switch to digital learning in a matter of days. The majority of schools, however, did not have adequate digital platforms to support online learning. So the problem statement is that the students and teachers were struggling. In order to offer a value proposition for education, it is required to identify what specific issues the education system is facing when the end-to-end learning and development process in K12 is considered. In terms of running the classes, the available videoconferencing platforms generated a quick and easy conversion; however, there was no quick replacement of quizzes and homework.

■ Step 2 — Ideate: As a second step, we concentrate on the specific issues and ideate around possible solutions. This step requires customer empathy, so the designer should think and act like the customer so techniques like mystery shopping (going through the experience like an actual customer and observing the requirements from first hand) or empathy mapping (the customers end to end journey map is driven from their emotions) are frequently used.

  Going back to the education example, after a period of ideation, digital document management companies came up with the online content editing solution and prototyped this front end to the market. These ideations require defining specific solutions for their personas (main target customers that are identified with certain commonalities) for an elementary class offer and will differ from a high school one.

■ Step 3 – Prototype & Step 4 Testing: Whichever brilliant solution is identified in the previous step, it needs to be built in a mockup or demo format, which will allow testing. These two steps are important due to validation of the opportunity, not by leaders in the board but directly by the customers.

It can be considered as the initial MVP, which allows experimenting with the customer. The customer delivers all the positive and negative feedback so that the team can decide on launching the actual production.

In the education case, during testing, it was realized that the content editing was useful but the teachers required all of the students in the class to virtually enter values to the same document, so a collaboration tool extension was added.

Although it is much easier to prototype and test with users around technological solutions, it applies to all sorts of new offerings. If it is a commercial which will be broadcasted on multiple channels, for instance, there will be substantial value if a small group hears the storyline.

■ Step 5 – Reiterate or redefine: The last step emphasizes the attitude of continuous iteration. Whatever digital learning tool was offered to the students and teachers, and assumed successful delivery, the teams can never stop producing better. So the 5th step acts as a bridge to initiate another round of design thinking [42, 43].

As a result, in the education system case, the software companies managed to identify and solve a real customer problem, and further improve it with iterations. The companies which are providing schools with a digital classroom platform during the pandemic with fast time to market extensions have little or no possibility to fail.

Benefits: As the example states, when all steps of design thinking are applied before deciding on launching a new offering, the marketing department no longer gambles with the business outcomes. What is proposed to the customers has already been designed based on the customers' insight, their needs and requirements, then the proposition has been tested with real customers and iterated based on their comments. In a way, the failure of risk is minimized with design thinking-based production design in any sector. If practiced well, applying the technique has a significantly positive effect on the revenue.

Similar effect also applies to the cost side since every penny invested in the idea is experimented so there is no sunk cost generated. Furthermore, the cost-based pricing is calculated realistically, and the customer pays for the real monetary value. If the idea proves to be wrong or not valid, it is either instantly pivoted or completely killed. In summary, the company has an ability to optimize use of its resources.

4.2.3.2 Marketing Communications

Marketing communications that we cover includes both mass and targeted marketing. Over the recent years, due to the incredible acceleration of digital marketing, the mass marketing communication was already on the diminishing curve. With the effect of the pandemic period, it will further leap into the new normal working environment. Since we underlined the importance of creating value propositions with the deep customer insight in the above section, it is equally critical to communicate the brand messages to the customers based on their profiles.

In the traditional marketing communication strategy planning, the marketing research as described above generates a general insight regarding mass segments of customers. For instance, an electronics retail company may find out that customers in the 30–40 age group in large cities prefer shopping for televisions in brick-and-mortar shops. This is such a huge number of people with very different needs and reasons for shopping that when they are aggregated in a common segment, the only driven conclusion is that this retail company should invest in shop distribution channels. However, the customers who are about to get married looking for their first TV as a couple may have completely different service needs than a bachelor investing in a larger screen size for his flat. Although they are in the same segment, their needs and service expectations are different. On top, the second customer is highly eligible for converting to online shopping (Figure 4.27).

In the agile way of marketing management, the customer demand is the only driving force. Since it is not possible to create a separate proposition to each customer subgroup, exploiting digital technologies to bring segmentation and related brand communication to a micro level is the emerging trend, which is referred to as personalization. If we were still living in a physical communication era, this would surely be close to impossible: you can't basically adapt the offerings of millions of customers and expect your commercial staff to be able to deliver that. However, the digitalization of the communication enables micro-segmentation and customizing offerings around the expectations [44].

These two types of customers with cumulative sets of information regarding their demographics, preferences and habits are referred to as personas. A marketing persona is a fictional representation of actual users, presenting the drivers of customer decisions, without understanding in-depth dynamics [45]. The underlying factors of personas may vary from demographics to emotions. As mentioned in the

Segment: Age 30-40 & Large city resident

Persona: Young couple to be married

Need: face to face service

Segment: Age 30-40 & Large city resident

Persona: A businessman shopping for a larger TV

Need: Ease of purchase

Figure 4.27   Customer segmentation example.

insight-driven customer propositions, the persona definition plays an important role in communicating the right offering to the right customer.

Case: Imagine an airline company, who is providing online airline ticketing services, where their customers need to login with their loyalty numbers in order to benefit from promotions and campaigns. The company has access to the demographic information provided by the customer during loyalty card issues and can identify all related information when the customer logins. The environment is a perfect match for personalization. The company can track all previous flight destinations to offer the promotions which would be matching customers' expectations. For instance, if the previous purchases of airline tickets are dated around January to February to Austria and Switzerland, it would be safe to assume that the customer is a skier and it would be wise to bring ski resort bundle offers to the landing page. Even further, the company can offer ski equipment charge promotion as an add-on service to increase their service charge revenue.

This trend has a major prerequisite which is using advanced technologies related to data analytics. In order to detect, mine and analyze all different types of data sets that belong to the customer profile, acquired from multiple channels (social media, web tracking, and physical interaction logs) companies need to invest in big data and analytics. Bigger the data set, deeper the level of personalization and better chance to improve the offerings via the responses.

Benefits: More the customer insight, deeper the expectation recognition and higher possibility of companies to offer propositions to respond to those needs means higher sales and revenue. So this is an approach directly linked to above line benefits and has an effect on the company P&L. Furthermore, the ability to respond to customer expectations is directly linked to customer loyalty to the brand. So it is wise to assume that personalization of company offerings, either in product form, services or pricing is going to be on the top of C level agenda in the upcoming years.

4.2.3.3 Product Portfolio Management

After using customer insight to design and deliver the responsive value propositions as a first step and as a second step communicating the offering messages in a personalized manner, the third step of the marketing cycle is to optimize the portfolio of products. Product portfolio management is the process of determining the optimal investment and focus mix of a company's products and services.

In classical portfolio management, each income generator product has its own financial statement, where the revenue is measured from the sales generated and cost is calculated as a combination of direct costs and indirect costs allocated with a measurement key. An example of product cost is social media launch campaign fees which are accounted under the product's record and an example of an indirect cost is the allocation of CRM system renewal costs to the product record with a predefined proportion. In this way, the profit and loss statement of a certain business unit is generated (Figure 4.28).

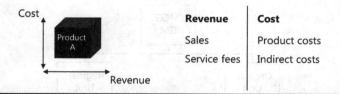

Figure 4.28   Product revenue and cost structure.

When this method is replicated for all products in the company portfolio, you end up with an aggregated P&L where each product is evaluated separately. As in line with any company's financial strategy, when the company's P&L is suffering due to shrinking market share or inefficient bottom line, top-down cost reduction actions are inevitable. As a result of this restructuring, both direct and indirect costs get a cut, and this cut affects all expenditures equally. The top-down cutting approach negatively affects all, even the segments of business that were on the growth path (Figure 4.29).

Case: Consider an FMCG company that is managed with traditional portfolio management. The company has two major production lines, which are organic and regular businesses. The organic line was created as a separate unit after increasing market demand and dedicated teams were formed under this unit. The regular line, which has been operating similarly for over 20 years, continued its operations in food and beverages categories (Figure 4.30).

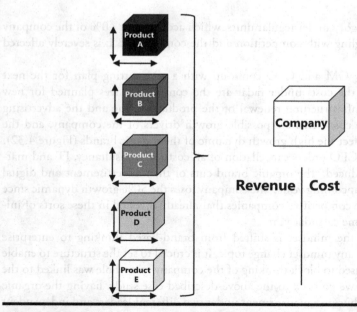

Figure 4.29   Product portfolio revenue and cost structure.

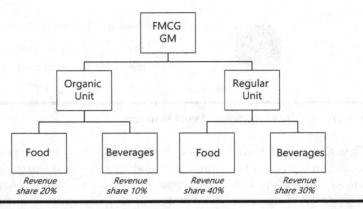

Figure 4.30 A sample FMCG company board structure.

Unit	Organic Food	Organic Beverage	Regular Food	Regular Beverage
Revenue share	20%	10%	40%	30%
Growth ratio	50%	40%	10%	30%

Figure 4.31 A sample FMCG company product categorization for revenue and growth ratios.

The food category under regular units, which accounts for 40% of the company revenue, is struggling with competition and the company P&L is severely affected (Figure 4.31).

The company GM and CFO come up with a cost-cutting plan for the next annual year and the costs under radar are the consultancy fees planned for new digital strategy, infrastructural renewal of the production line and the advertising budget. All these cost items are possible growth drivers of the company, and the cuts negatively affect the high growth dynamic of the organic brands (Figure 4.32).

So when the CFO orders cancellation of all costs, all consultancy, IT and marketing opex is reduced. The organic brand cuts of their advertisement and digital activities for the upcoming years. The company loses the 50% growth dynamic since it falls behind the competitive companies that already invested in these sorts of initiatives for the same calendar year.

With agility, the mindset is shifted from brand-based thinking to enterprise thinking. As with any mindset change topic, it is crucial to set the structure to enable this shift. What used to block thinking of the company as a whole was linked to the silo structures. If we go back to the above-described case study, having the organic and non-organic business management under two different leaders and independent teams result in completely separate strategic planning per brand. However, if the food

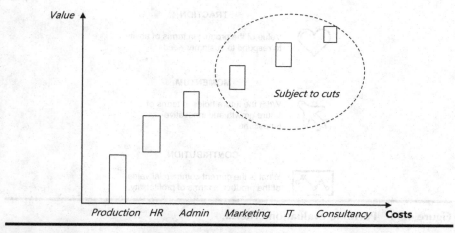

Figure 4.32 A sample value versus cost table of main company costs.

line of a regular unit fails, it is a company failure, and due to the share of revenue, this segment can even risk the sustainability of the company in the market. Removing the silos by agile organizational alignment as explained in the organizational agility chapter and uniting the company under holistic company goals as explained in agile finance management enables the collaborative business environment.

The methodology that supports the transition is enterprise portfolio prioritization. In this method, all the revenue generators are united under one portfolio basket view and evaluated with respect to the dimensions related to the product. The criteria supported by MIT Sloan research is three dimensional:

- Traction is the value of the product to its customers, it's high if it serves an unmet need or if it's a product that customers advocate for,
- Momentum is looking toward the future and defining whether the product is a growth driver or whether the company is investing in a pipeline to develop the product even more and
- Contribution is examining the current market value, the positioning among the competition and ratio of profitability [46].

When all three layers which include several related sub-layers are combined, we can define the priority of the product in direct comparison to all the rest in the portfolio (Figure 4.33). This allows us to analyze the integrated outlook of the whole enterprise in a single picture. This view makes synergic decision-making on the strategic actions possible.

Case: In order to understand the structure better, we can go back to the FMCG company case as described above (Figure 4.34).

There are five types of products in the company, which belong to four different business units. The distribution of products to units is as illustrated in the above

TRACTION

Value of the product in terms of ability
to respond to customer needs

MOMENTUM

What the future holds in terms of
future growth and innovative
landscape

CONTRIBUTION

What is the current commercial value
of the product in terms of profitability

Figure 4.33   Portfolio evaluation criteria.

Unit	Organic Food	Organic Beverage	Regular Food	Regular Beverage
Products	C	E	D, B	A

Figure 4.34   Product categorization table of a sample FMCG company.

table. Since the regular food line corresponding to the company revenue is the largest, they have two different types of products served to their customers.

In order to apply a cross comparison analysis of the three- layered criteria, traction, momentum and contribution, it is required to assess each of the five products with the same lens and plot the numeric outcomes in a single three-dimensional chart, as illustrated in Figure 4.35.

In the below representation, the X-axis is the measure of momentum, the Y-axis is the traction level and the bubble size refers to the contribution, so larger the diameter, the product sales contribute more to the company revenue. It is possible to observe that the organic line products, C and E, promise high levels of return for the near future since they are on the far-right area of the momentum axis. The products D and B both are under the responsibility of the regular food line, where B is the lowest value generator among all and D is still bringing income with a less optimistic future. The regular beverage A doesn't promise a strong pipeline but the current product on the market is a love brand of customers with the highest traction.

After the comparative status is analyzed, the Product Managers of four lines come together to propose corrective actions:

■ Product A: Although no new significant investment is expected, due to customer's loyalty and steady revenue generation the product is kept on the shelf, however, with less marketing expense.

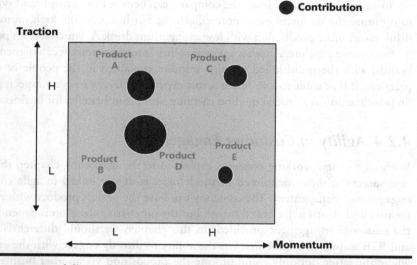

Figure 4.35   Portfolio evaluation criteria chart of a sample FMCG company.

- Product B: This product has the lowest value in terms of all variables and is doomed to fail, so the product is terminated.
- Product C: Even though the current contribution is not the largest, with very high traction and most promising momentum, C will be the rock to rely on. The funds of Product B and partial funds of Product A to be converted to this product.
- Product D: Backbone of the company P&L, top contributor to revenue with an intermediate traction and momentum value. The resources invested will be kept flat.
- Product E: Although carriers have high potential, the traction is very low so targeted marketing investment to increase customer loyalty is planned.

As a result, the company manages the actions per brand on a zero-sum basis, there is no need to cut back on growth investment but rather adjust the cost allocated to regressive brands and even sunsetting some products.

Benefits: Application of this method is crucial to effective management of company resources, so there is a direct link to company bottom line optimization and also an indirect advantage caused by the ability to invest in growth potential even in turbulent times. In addition to all, the company management has full transparency of the whole portfolio in an integrated manner and can easily shift marketing strategy as a response to external or internal disruptions.

From a different lens, there is also the gained opportunity cost due to not cutting expenses linked to growth that would put the high momentum brands behind the competition.

On a further maturity level, the company can benefit from cross brand synergies to optimize the resources even more efficiently. For instance, the high momentum drink E can unite production with low momentum drink A, which has no possibility to improve pipeline. Another synergy ability is to share resources assigned to the brands, with the multiskilled peoples' mindset explained in the people & culture practices, it is possible to join forces across expertise. Hereby in every aspect, portfolio prioritization is a crucial method carrying significant benefits for business.

4.2.4 Agility in Customer Engagement

With all the new working concepts explained in the marketing chapter, the business success of these mentioned methodologies is tightly linked to agile customer engagement management. The company can have the perfect product with premier features and an attractive brand image, but the purchasing decision is dependent on the customer engagement provided. In this chapter, we should differentiate B2C and B2B sectors where the first has the ability to directly engage with the end user where the latter can only communicate the proposition via another business. The model we mark is more appropriate to B2C models and has limited implications for B2B businesses.

In order to understand all dynamics of agile customer engagement, we have a deeper look into how the go-to-market strategy is formed if the customer is in the center of the process, then how the sales targets are adjusted and finally how the internal governance of the field teams should be, to allow new ways of working.

4.2.4.1 Customer-Oriented Go-To-Market

Large-scale companies, with a significant sales force, build their go-to-market strategies based on their organizational structure and the underlying products and services. When the company grows in the number of customers and offer a greater variety of propositions, they tend to add new representatives and units to their sales force. With this continuing approach, companies with long presence in their respective markets, end up having more than one representative serving a single customer. Having multiple engagement partners for a customer causes certain drawbacks. The root cause is related to having a silo-based management structure, where the customer-facing roles have different communication strategies and business priorities. Generally, these conflicts of interest are reflected to the customer.

Case: A common example for this topic is multinational banks' engagement model. In general, banks operate under customer segment silos, which are retail, commercial and corporate. They also segment services like branch tellers and contact center representatives. So a customer who has multiple types of accounts with the bank may easily have interactions with more than one contact. Assuming a customer's journey: in a morning visit to the branch, interacts with the teller when making a cash transaction, then sees her retail account rep for opening a personal

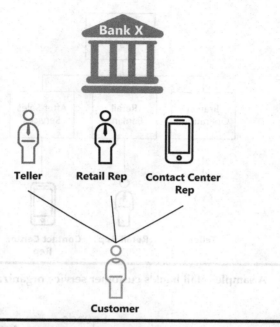

Figure 4.36   A sample retail bank's customer engagement chart.

savings account and on the way back from the branch receives a contact center call (Figure 4.36).

The handicap of this engagement system is that each point of contact of the bank has a different background knowledge and communication experience with the customer. The retail rep has provided the customer an attractive interest rate for his savings account which made the customer very satisfied until receiving a sales call from the contact center on the way to his home, offering a higher interest rate for her savings. The customer was frustrated with the contradicting messages and offerings. On top, she loses trust of the branch sales rep, who has been serving her for many years.

In agile customer engagement, the factor that shapes the design of the go-to-market model is not the product. As explained in the marketing chapter, the customer becomes the center of the interaction map, and all designs evolved around it. The root cause of the above-stated issue is the fact that the three different contacts report to different managerial lines: teller is working under branch operations, retail rep is reporting to retail banking and finally the contact center reports to after-sales services (Figure 4.37).

Since with an agile way of working the organizational structuring is liberated from the border of silos, the head office structure evolves into a squad system – as illustrated a possible retail customer tribe may include squads dedicated to offering streamlined propositions for new products developed, supported by after-sales

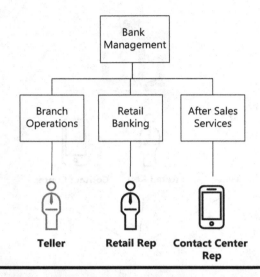

Figure 4.37 A sample retail bank's customer service organization structure.

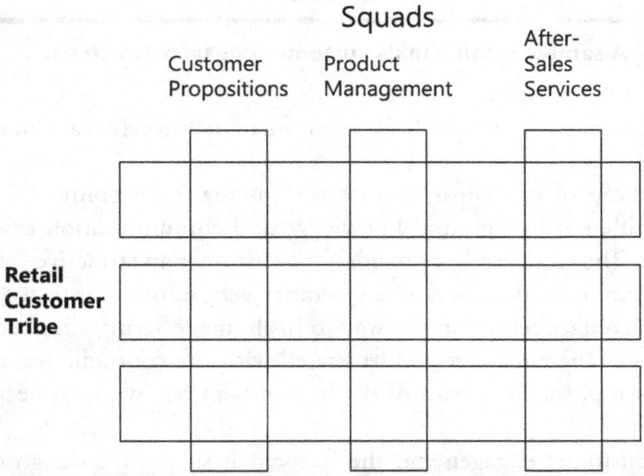

Squads

	Customer Propositions	Product Management	After-Sales Services
Retail Customer Tribe			

Figure 4.38 A sample agile organization chart for a retail bank.

services. These squads work in coordination to optimize the end-to-end customer experience in the retail banking area. These strategic designs directly feed into the customer-facing teams to be delivered to the customer (Figure 4.38).

In parallel, the customer-facing staff is reorganized in order to provide a seamless service to the customer. As an important step, the primary point of contact concept is introduced in engagement management. The three customer-facing roles are united as a single representative, serving every demand of the customer. This way

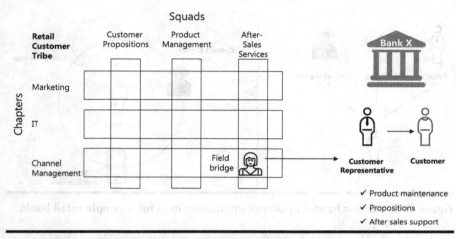

Figure 4.39   A sample agile service model for a retail bank.

the bank has a 360-degree view of the customer journey and can provide the best service (Figure 4.39).

In order to build the flow of information between the squad and the branches, a member of the channel management or sales chapter takes on bridging responsibility. She coordinates the workflows, transfers narratives of newly designed products or re-engineers a service process based on branch feedback.

The approach also applies to companies that have a leaner interaction model with customers since almost all sectors have built multiple channels with the abilities of digitalization. So even a video streaming company can create customer dissatisfaction due to conflicting offers coming from e-mail offers and what call centers offer during subscription extension calls.

The only way to target the root cause of the issue is to be able to have a single view of the customer, which is dependent on building an omnichannel customer management platform attached to the company's customer relationship management application. Omnichannel engagement is a business approach, where all access channels of customer journey are synchronized and assumes the process which starts in one channel and continues in another following the same structure [47] (Figure 4.40).

Illustrating the concept with our case analysis, the bank converting the primary contact structure and aligning all communication and offerings with an integrated communication platform and allowing a single view of the customer generates a seamless interaction with the customer.

Benefits: As mentioned at the beginning of this chapter, both marketing and customer engagement adoption to agility imply significant business benefits. The above-stated approach to customer engagement ensures customer's brand loyalty and high satisfaction with the field representative, who is in a way the face of the company.

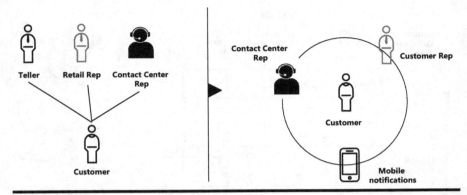

Figure 4.40   Omnichannel customer interaction map for a sample retail bank.

Surely, the loyalty and satisfaction converge into numbers. According to Dimension Data's 2017 Global Customer Experience Benchmarking Report, which addresses 1,351 organizations in 80 counties, 84% of the organizations realized revenue improvement after applying improvements in customer experience [48]. What is interesting though is with 71% of organizations claiming that CX is their top priority, just 13% of them rate their delivery a nine out of ten or better. So it is very clear that the revenue implications are only possible if the actions are executed, and the outcome is perceived on the customers' end.

4.2.4.2 Sales Target Management

After defining the ideal go-to-market strategy, the next step is to plan sales targets effectively. In the classical sales planning approach, the sales leaders set a solid account planning for the upcoming year, parallel to the financial planning cycle, sign and seal the plan and lead their teams to act with respect to this plan completely. The similar timing to the financial planning cycle is no coincidence since the top-down company financial targets convert into the sales plans.

Since the financial planning, as explained also in agility in finance chapter, delivers the target figures for all components: the revenue to be generated from products, – if it is a service company – revenue from service charges, the sales amount expected from each channel: breakdown of targets for physical and digital channels, and even in some cases targets for new or existing customers can be defined top-down (Figure 4.41).

Case: Let's assume an air conditioning retailer, called Cool, which earns revenue from sales of products and services. There are three types of products they merchandise: split conditioner, heating system and air purifier and provide two types of services: maintenance and filter cleaning. At the end of 2020, the Finance Department of Cool presents the 2021 expected sales and the breakdown of total revenue, which is 110m $. There is an additional channel target stating that 40%

Financial Targets	T + 1 year	T + 2 years	T + 3 years
Product Revenue	100		
Product A	40		
Physical Channel	30		
Digital Channel	10		
.....			
Services Revenue	50		
Service X	30		
Physical Channel	20		
Digital Channel	10		
.....			

Figure 4.41   A sample company target table.

Cool Company ($)	Sales Target	Region 1 Target	Sales Rep Target
Product Revenue	80	35	3.5
Split conditioner	40	20	2
Heating system	30	10	1
Air purifier	10	5	0.5
Services Revenue	30	6	0.6
Maintenance	20	4	0.4
Filter cleaning	10	2	0.2

Figure 4.42   Cool company target table.

of product revenue, which is 32m $, should come from online sales. This figure was 16m $ in the previous year so the expectation is doubling revenue on e-commerce (Figure 4.42).

The company operates in four different regions around the country, so there are four regional managers in the organization chart, who report to the sales director. The customer engagement team in the Cool shops are distributed among the four regions and directly report to their respective regional manager. After the CFO presents the annual targets to the sales director, she gathers her direct reports to give the annual targets, in a proportion to four regions (Figure 4.43).

The first region, which is covering the capital and large cities, is a key region to deliver the targets, so they get the higher proportion of all. Since there is no rejection culture on a given target, the Region 1 sales manager accepts the challenge and gathers her team to explain their expectations. The region is made up of 10 sales representatives, and they have equal division of their region targets, so the sales Rep X gets the following personal targets. These numbers simply mean that the

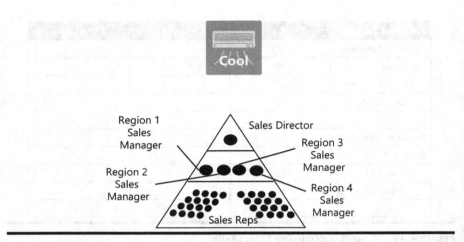

Figure 4.43 Cool company customer engagement organization structure.

premium he will get out of the annual performance cycle is dependent on whether he achieves 4.1m $ (3.5m $ sales from products and 0.6m $ from services) during the year. Since the sales department premium to wage ratio is usually around 60% to 40% (60% fixed wage and 40% variable pay) the premium income is a critical portion of his salary.

What Rep X will do all through the year will be then focused entirely on selling and what he will call a success in achieving the 4.1m $ sales. Naturally, when a customer enters the shop, he will try to persuade the shopper with a tell-and-sell method. HBR calls this being obsessed with the compensation system [49]. Plus, if it is the month of December and his numbers are still staggering around 3m, he will apply the hard sell technique, which is scaring the shopper into buying [50]. These techniques lead to dissatisfied customers and although they may have purchased the air conditioner, they would never step a foot in that shop again. In a 2019 State of Sales Study conducted by Salesforce Company, 79% of buyers say it is absolutely critical to interact with a salesperson who is a trusted advisor, not just a sales rep [51]. Another handicap of the model is that, if a commercial customer makes a 4m $ purchase in January, the Rep X has no motivation to generate more through the year. The reason behind this behavior is ratcheting quotas, where the company increases the quota for the rep or the team if they overperform through the year [52].

Whereas in agile sales management, the field teams do not have top-down financial targets which are strictly divided in order to figure individual targets. Instead, their performance is measured with the value they generate through each quarter. Some companies also prefer to change the fixed to variable pay ratios accordingly but that is not a prerequisite. With the pressure of over-concentrating on hitting personal sales targets released, the sales reps are expected to focus on outcomes. As explained with the OKR concept, the sales is an output, it surely is a positive output for the company's financial statement but it is not an outcome. However, customer satisfaction is an outcome that promises sustainability or in other words guarantee future growth.

If we go back to the Cool Company case, having adapted agile sales management methodologies, changes the targets to ambitions. As illustrated in the below table, the company presents the sales teams, some reference data to create the business ambition, some examples showing average sale per rep as a benchmark, or comparing the company reps with the biggest competitors, or if it is an international company, with a close-range peer country office performance. This way the field is not target bounded. There is no need to push the customer who enters the store to buy a split conditioner to rather purchase an air purifier since his target for the split is already met. When the subcategory performance pressure is released, the performance pay becomes how much the salesperson X has achieved retrospectively when compared to his peers.

Also, in order to ensure the achieved revenue was performed by ensuring customer satisfaction, the retailers initiate a quick customer survey after the delivery, asking the customer to rate the retailer and measure the net promoter score. Making customer service teams responsible for customer satisfaction significantly changes the approach toward customers (Figure 4.44).

Adjusting sales targets is a useful tool to help sales teams to adapt to agile working but the behavioral and skill set adaptation surely takes longer. In order to understand which types of behavior needs to change, it is useful to have an overview of new principles of selling [53]:

■ **Listening:** First and foremost, the sales force needs to concentrate on improving their listening capabilities. The general tell-and-sell approach emphasizes talking and persuasion ability. I am sure any reader can confirm that the most

Cool Company ($)	Previous Year sales	Region 1 PY sales	Avg per rep sales	Top Competitor PY sales	NPS Score
Product Revenue	60	25	2.5	4	
Split conditioner	30	10	1	2	
Heating system	20	10	1	1	
Air purifier	10	5	0.5	1	6.5
Services Revenue	20	5	0.5	0.7	
Maintenance	10	3	0.3	0.4	
Filter cleaning	10	2	0.1	0.3	

Figure 4.44   Cool company target breakdown per products and services.

common capability of a salesperson is being silver-tongued, which in general comes with a side effect of not being the best listener. The listening is not for building conversations, which is of course important, but rather to capture needs, expectations or complaints and not to jump into a sales pitch. This would help to build a trust.

■ **Preparation:** If the company representative and customer interaction is a planned one, like an agreed visit to their office, the preparation phase is also very important. As we have mentioned in the single view of the customer database description, the representative should make use of all available data, obtain useful insight about the customer and pre-shape the pitch accordingly.

■ **Pitching:** During the actual pitch, it is more sensible to focus on giving guidance about the value of the product or the service, with a narrative instantly customized in accordance with the unmet need of the customer.

Benefits: As mentioned at the beginning of the chapter, with agile methods the company can remove the barriers of number focused sales approach toward relationship building. This will ensure continuation of the representative and customer relationship, whether it is a B2C or B2B2C business.

The customers who are not pushed but pulled to the products or services the company provides become loyal to the brand. If the representative is also able to perform deep listening and understand the real needs of the customer, the bond to the brand will be stronger.

In a previous experience, I was responsible for the customer engagement in a business line and the customer reports showed that single purchasers were dominating the frequent buyers. To overcome this, we have conducted a sales satisfaction survey call series to first-time buyers, and we have asked how satisfied the customers were with the products they have purchased. A vast majority of the surveyed customers responded saying they were not really planning to buy that product but the customer representative insisted so they purchased but haven't used it yet. They also graded low for a possibility to buy any other product from our company in the future which means the one-time purchase did not bring any benefit to the company and affected negatively in the long run.

Another positive implication of loyalty is surely the word-of-mouth effect, which describes the targeted efforts of customers sharing their positive feedback with others. According to Nielsen's 2012 Global Trust in Advertising Report, which surveyed more than 28,000 responders in 56 countries, 92% respond that they value recommendations from friends or family above all forms of advertising [54].

So a company taking the agile business management path, should not exclude the alteration approach to sales target management. Removing sales targets should not be understood as having no control or tracking over the sales but rather building a flexible mechanism to make sure the sales force acts in the best interest of the customer.

4.2.4.3 Sales Organization Coordination

With the go-to-market strategy and the tactics plan including the target setting structure is defined, the next and final step in the sales management cycle is to design the internal coordination mechanism so that the plan is also executed efficiently.

The sales teams in enterprises with a large field force are organized in respective to their managerial structures. Bigger the scale of the company more fragmented is the organizational set-up. In almost all sectors I have consulted, the sales distribution is based on regions, which means the geographical divisions among the country. So the direct report to the Chief Sales Officer are the Regional Heads, representing the cities under their territory. When the company has a different variety of products or services that need special attention, there is further division on the N-2 level in accordance with the groups of products.

Case: A valid example to consider would be an insurance company; since they serve a wide variety of products and services ranging from protecting customers health, wealth and all sorts of belongings. Each of these elements has different riskiness criteria, so requires separate processes for offering or pricing. The possibility of financial damage caused by a car crash in a metropolitan is triple the risk of loss due to theft of a house in a secure neighborhood. In addition, although the e-commerce ratio is growing in recent years, the business is still very much based on face-to-face sales, so the field structure should provide reasonable proximity. An average large-scale insurance company would have a sales and service structure similar to the below graphic (Figure 4.45).

In this case study, the Secure insurance company consists of two main sections: the sales team is divided into three regions with regional manager's direction, and each region has two team leads that are managing teams dedicated to Property & casualty products and Life & Pension products. On the right-hand side, there is a small structure of the after-sales team managed by a separate director, however, again organized in the same regional structure. The services only apply to the P&C business, so there is no further team breakdown under regions. Finally, the different shapes placed under the organization chart, refer to the teams working with this management structure.

The main obstacle produced by this chart is the vertical information flow: since the targets (as explained in the above section) divides the sales team, as well as geography, the only way of information flow is upward or downward. In daily life of P&C team 1, closing their second quarter of sales, they work reporting on their achievements, which are combined by P&C Team Lead 1, to be further integrated to the numbers coming from the L&P team similarly, all ending up on the Region 1 Manager. Then all are combined on a national level to be viewed by the Chief Sales Officer. The service team repeats a similar task so that the CEO can have a single-paged chart representing the company performance. So the upward information flow is about achievements and performance status, and the downward message transfer is only regarding the targets and strategic direction (Figure 4.46).

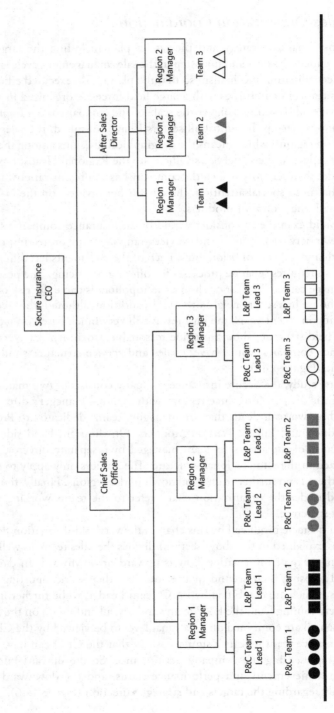

Figure 4.45 A sample insurance company service organization.

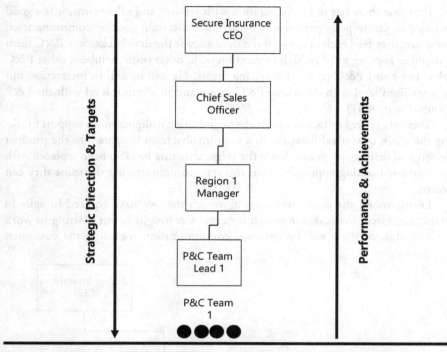

Figure 4.46   Management structure of a sample P&C insurance team.

On top of all, there is no horizontal communication. The tree structure provides a certain Chinese wall between products and regions. Since there is no room for collaboration, the vertical transfer of messages seems sufficient to all parties involved.

However, the ore is hidden in the minds of the customer-facing teams. Whether they are selling or servicing, only they have direct connection to the customers, so they collect all these precious insights and feedback constantly. If they are asked, they very well know the impediments of the company's servicing processes, the competitive pricing and also the core reasons why customers prefer them. However, this information is unstructured and lost since they are not captured in corporate memory.

In agile sales structuring, the organizational alignment is much leaner. Inclusion of the primary point of contact and single view of customer concepts create the base, but there is also room for improvement in the internal communication. In comparison with the previous version of the organization structure, you may notice that the sales and services are united to ensure a single view of the customer is achieved and one level of hierarchy removed to enable leaner flow of requirements. Another major change is breaking the walls of the regional boundaries; whichever city the customer lives in, the proposition or the quality of service she will get should be the same, so that the sales strategy should be aligned across the country.

If in case there has to be a separation with services and sales teams, it is a good practice to create pods per region, which have a certain routine communication cycle that they feed each other with the dynamics or the drawbacks. So a P&C team 1 member is going to be in high interaction with: other team members, other P&C sales teams and P&C region 1 servicing teams. He will be still in interaction but in a medium level with the whole P&C group and in a minor level with the L&P group (Figure 4.47).

There are other key factors beside the organizational alignment to support breaking the chain of vertical flow: the first is to involve team insights into the product design and delivery processes. Since the target structure has also been replaced with an outcome tracking approach, the teams start communicating the value they can create.

Furthermore, the design thinking approach that we have covered in agile in marketing forces the teams to search for customer insight before starting to work on any idea, so there will be constant communication regarding the customer.

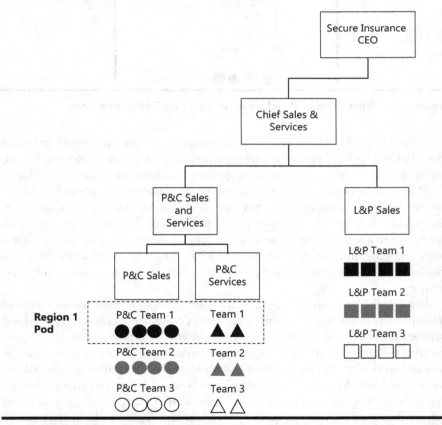

Figure 4.47 Sample agile insurance company organization service model.

In a way, the field force in the agile model is the source of customer initiatives; they constantly discover customer unmet needs through relationship building and deep listening and carry these insights to initiate progressive actions with business teams.

Companies should provide the field forces with systems that enable capturing these valuable insights and converting them to projects. Global CRM solutions support custom developed front ends where the field staff enters initiatives, on the same system the customer visits are recorded. In addition, having the customer engagement force also involved in the project design and execution phases will support correct prototyping as well as internalization of the customer-centric culture.

Benefits: When we create a structure that allows transparency of all company information, we reduce the risk of blind-sidedness substantially. This way, the board, sales managers, the finance teams and risk management department all have a clearer view of dynamics in the market. The insight from the end user and competition will definitely be a key driver for the marketing teams, designing the offers that customers will desire so that there is also a direct effect on the top line.

If we think of the money and effort spent on countrywide surveys, brand-based market research, focus group analysis etc. to gather insights from customers, it is interesting that the best source of information is rather overlooked.

Beyond all, the field teams' motivational status is affected very positively, after accepting the status of an extension team only forced more sales in long years, being a part of the strategic planning gives them higher job satisfaction. Also, if they are given the responsibility to deliver those projects as well, the motivation and sense of belonging are positively affected.

4.2.5 Agile Risk and Compliance Management

Organizations are built on governance structures that include processes and procedures to ensure it works as planned. The governing body, which is the management, takes ownership of organizational oversight and implements lines of defense to secure the company from internal and external risks. In order to manage those risks closely, a three lines defense model is used.

In the first line of defense, the managerial roles carry the responsibility of implementing and applying internal measures. In the second life of defense, control teams are responsible for implementing correct checkpoints and measures to minimize the risk. In the last line of defense, internal audit, which is an independent body reporting to the board, has the right to audit all units and lines of defenses and offer corrective actions on findings. This solid structure and division of responsibilities ensure minimizing occurrence of risk and if for cases where the risk arises, early intervention is to have minor effect on the company [55].

As business models evolve, organizations grow, and technological advances introduce new channels, the companies become more risk prone. The control of occurrence had to multiply to be able to track all these dynamics. As a result, the owners of three lines of defenses concentrate on implementing an increased number of mitigating actions and precautions.

While this is the case, agile transformations' effect on reshaping internal processes and structures to enable leaner management and faster execution surely raises questions regarding the risk and compliance management. Since risk management processes are less complex compared to other support functions the main shift is not related to the structure but rather the approach of risk management.

4.2.5.1 Internal Control

First line of defense relies on managerial measures to eliminate the operational risk at its maximum. In order to achieve this, hierarchical organizations implement various systematic control steps. The most common are escalation and four eyes control principles, which are used in monetary transactions.

Case: Banking transactions is a typical example of this sort. A bank operations expert cannot directly process a $ 500K payment. The hierarchy in the organization delivers a safety net to ensure the correct process applies, so the EFT is controlled by three or four different members of the organization. After the entry of payments details by expert 1, the second expert rechecks the entry, which is called the four eyes principle. The four eyes principle is favored since the controls do not create operational burden on managerial lines. Then the managerial roles check the entry furthermore, until the last control is completed by the director, and the payment is ready to be transferred to the customer's account.

There are three issues related to the flow: first, assigning the EFT to higher management does not guarantee healthier analysis of the transaction, when compared to the specialist who has maximum hands-on experience; second, the process is too lengthy so probably ends up with customer getting the payment 3 days later and is disappointed with the company and last this doesn't represent the most efficient use of time value of a company.

In an agile way of internal control, the system is the key to minimize risk involving monetary operations management. The companies that apply the agile methodologies convert their human-centric control mechanisms to automated systems. There are types of modern technology which makes the job easy like rule engine-based process re-engineering systems and the RPA.

In order to clarify this point, a visualization of the technology would be supportive. In the below illustration, there is a screenshot of an EFT screen with rules engine automation. There, the controls that the payment specialist should perform before confirming a payment are system checked, and the results are shown to take further action (Figure 4.48).

In the initial scenario, all of the rules are verified by the system due to the controls implemented (example: making sure the entry details are sufficient and the account is available for such a transaction and also checking the compliance rules where additional risk may be involved). In this case, the RPA allows the EFT numbered

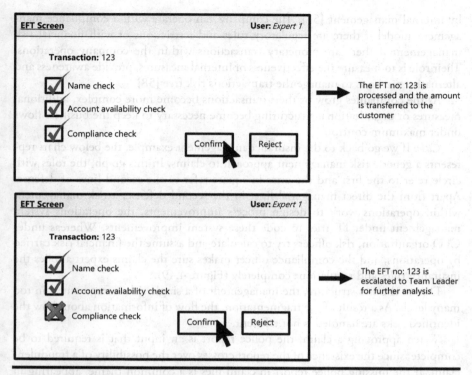

Figure 4.48   A sample EFT process of a bank.

123 to be confirmed and directly processed, without further escalation. However, in the second scenario, represented by the second-page illustration, the compliance check isn't verified, which may arise from a late payment that creates a blockage in the senders' account, and in this case, if expert 1 misses further check and confirms the payment, this time the transaction is automatically escalated to the Team Leader to take corrective action.

Benefits: Converging the control from people to the system is much more risk averse than the escalation procedure. Although the previous version may seem more secure since there are a couple of steps to complete a payment, the efficiency and attention over the cases decrease as it is escalated to higher management. In addition, the end-to-end process is significantly shortened which also has a positive effect on the customer satisfaction since customers value the length of services as a key identifier [56].

4.2.5.2 Risk Management

The second line refers to a variety of risk management functions, which aim to implement frameworks, policies and tools to minimize the risk that cannot be eliminated by internal management [57]. The company can operate with a compliance management model if there are regulatory rules and restrictions or with financial risk management if there are monetary transactions within the company operations. Their role is to measure the effectiveness of internal measures, provide awareness and alternative methods to manage the transactions risk free [58].

As the companies grow or their transactions become more complex, additional measures or organizational structuring become necessary to keep the business flows under maximum control.

Case: If we go back to the insurance management example, the below chart represents a generic risk management approach to claims. In this graph, the roles with circle refer to the first and the ones in square refer to the second lines of defense. Apart from the direct managerial line, in the second defense, a risk management within operations work to design process improvements, the operations system management under IT tries to code these system improvements. Whereas under CFO organization, risk officers try to calculate and assume the financial risk carried by operations, and the compliance officer makes sure the claims expert applies the insurance rules and regulations completely (Figure 4.49).

Due to the silo structure, the management of a single risk is fragmented in too many levels. As a result of the fragmentation, the flow of information about how the identified risks are handled is not efficient.

When approving a claim, the police report is an input that is required to be complete, since the existence of the report crosses over the possibility of a fraudulent claim. If the missing police report in claim files is a common theme, appearing in high-value claims, the second line of defense may be notified about the case via an audit report and separately start working on corrective actions. The CRO line tries to calculate the possible miss payments financial amount, where the compliance officer creates a report to the regulative body to report the event. In parallel, the operations risk manager tries to implement new procedures and deliver training. All these actions are not synchronized and since they are independent initiatives they do not serve a common objective.

Whereas in agile risk management, the units who work to minimize the risk in the process flow gather around a squad structure and work through preventive measures rather than post-event actions (Figure 4.50).

As can be seen in the above illustration, the claims management lines of motor and non-motor converge into motor and non-motor claims squads where representatives from all risk management teams are distributed among the squads to work together on a common strategy and objective: to minimize the risk. On the one hand, if the department that transfers resources has a dedicated member to the squad, i.e. the motor system expert versus the non-motor system expert; that person becomes a full-time member of the core squad. On the other hand, if the department has a unique expert, serving the topic of more than one squad, then the member becomes a shared resource and divides his time between related squads, based on the need and work plans; i.e. compliance and financial risk specialist in this case.

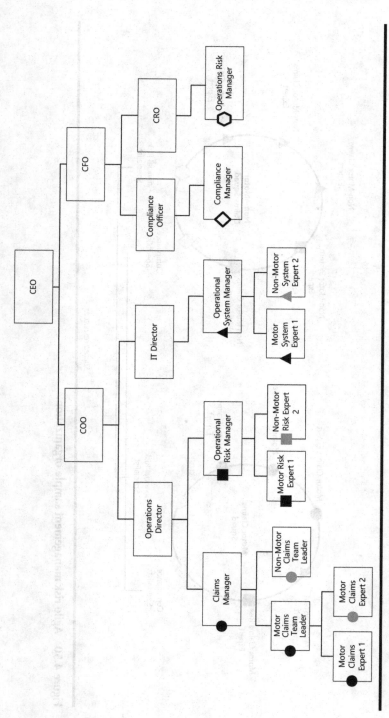

Figure 4.49 Risk management organization in a sample insurance company.

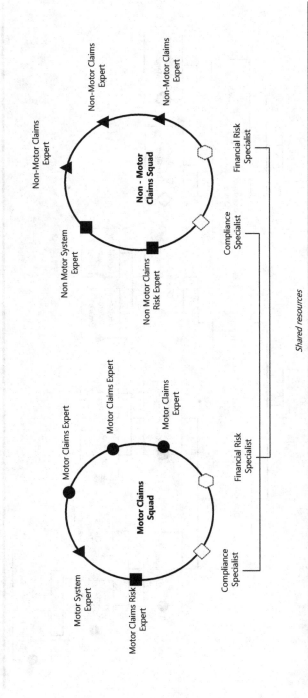

Figure 4.50   Agile risk management sample organization.

Benefits: Among all benefits, the coordination around different units with similar objectives is the key. The objective has always been the same, however, on the one hand, fragmenting the target to so many levels in silos made departments take on independent tasks on themselves. The agile model on the other hand enables merged first and second line of defense, they can work in a coherent manner. This is definitely more targeted when compared to different units and resources dedicated. So there is an efficiency benefit attached to it. Finally, the financial implications of risks can lead to company bankruptcies so effective risk management has a positive impact on the P&L. So a combined and integrated first and second line of control, leveraging system checking technologies leaves less risk for the third line of defense.

4.2.5.3 Internal Audit

The last resort in lines of defenses is the internal audit, an independent unit, reporting to the board directly, providing assurance on effectiveness of governance and controls. As the Institute of Internal Auditors (IIA) defines, the unit is responsible for bringing a system to ensure discipline to internal processes and effectively manage the organizational risk [59].

In terms of organizational design, the audit function must have an independent position in the company, which is assured of having a separate reporting line to the highest reporting body, in many cases directly to the CEO or if exists, to the advisory board. This structuring ensures the right to investigate any unit in the company, without going through a bureaucratic information flow and also unquestioned access to all company data.

The processes that the audits are executed are defined by the IIA and generally common among companies [60]. There are four main steps to complete an audit, which are:

- *Planning:* The audit team performs a preliminary analysis of the department that is planned to be audited with different tools like surveys or data analysis. With the help of this analysis, the possible risks are identified and the related department is notified with the upcoming audit program.
- *Fieldwork:* Depending on the department investigated the method of fieldwork may differ, varying from one-to-one interviews, secret customer observations, data scouting and analysis.
- *Reporting:* Involves a draft report where the audited unit declares corrective actions to overcome risk-bearing areas, which is followed by submission of the final report. This report carries vital importance since it is the declaration of the business unit confirming their efforts to take mitigating actions.
- *Follow up:* This step is closely related to the reporting stage since the auditor has the right to re-audit the processes declared risky in the report and check on the continuation of the corrective actions (Figure 4.51).

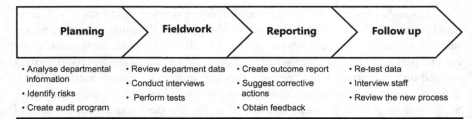

Figure 4.51   Internal audit process flow.

Although the above-explained process is highly standardized and structured, as is the case with all managerial topics we have covered, it was required to evolve with the new way of working approaches and the pace of the changing business. The foremost concern is the duration: a typical audit process in a large corporation can easily take up to six months to be completed. The main reason for lengthiness is the fieldwork, which is elongated due to back-and-forth analysis, requiring additional data along the way and analyzing all available data. The second reason is the reporting phase where the report has been tried to bring to perfection, trying to present all findings, including all possible actions to overcome the risks. The implication of the lengthy time is also the resources allocated, the people working on completion of the audit are numerous, not only from the audit team but also from the business units and even the teams from the second line of defense.

In the new approach to auditing, the very formal and predefined structure is amended in order to allow adapting to the constantly changing internal environment. The rigid process of audit, where the actions are consecutive and dependent on the previous step is altered to be more interrelated and flexible. The flow chart itself turns into a cycle where many steps of multiple audits can proceed simultaneously (Figure 4.52).

The new process basically has 6 steps:

- *Audit backlog:* Converting the structured planning phase to a backlog of audit activities, with the related audit team and key stakeholders. The user stories within the backlog define which certain tests are needed to be performed across the organization. The backlog is subject to change within the calendar year according to the emerging risks around the business topics.
- *Definition of ready:* This refers to the initiation efforts of the audit, involving the auditors and the stakeholders, agreeing on the inputs that are going to be examined.
- *Audit sprints:* Actual execution of the audit, within sprint logic, with sections of completed investigations, acting as minimum viable products. These activity intervals, which can be weekly or biweekly, involve a heavy dedication and strict compliance to the timeboxed activities. The business unit audited also

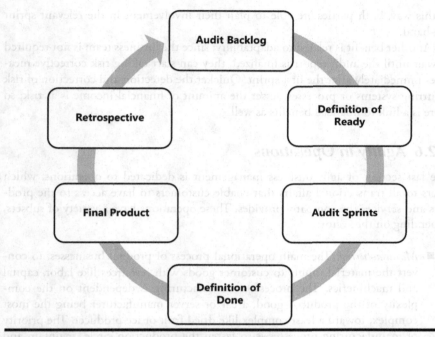

Figure 4.52   Agile internal audit management cycle.

comply with the timebox and provide the required data, input or interviews in the shortest time [61].

■ *Definition of done:* DoD represents the outputs of the sprints, although the scope of a single sprint is much narrower than a traditional audit report, it is sufficient to underline key points to consider.

■ *Final product:* A combination of sprints refer to the final product, where the accumulated view of individual sprints form a point of view document. The corrective actions regarding the sprint findings do not require waiting until the final product is ready [62].

■ *Sprint retrospective:* As similar to an end to any sort of scrum approach, the agile audit teams gather after closing a final product, to review the outcomes and evaluate the working dynamics to improve the process even better.

Benefits: The benefits of adapted auditing are first and foremost efficiency. The approach is more efficient in terms of time, as explained the current rigid structure of auditing takes months for a single department's audit report to be generated. The elongated time intervals create a work burden both to auditors and to the business team constantly supporting them as well. In the new model, the slices of audit topics are distributed to sprints and each sprint has certain stakeholders to engage with;

in this way, both parties are able to plan their involvement in the relevant sprint pre-hand.

Another benefit is related to adaptability; since the business team is not required to wait until the audit report is finalized, they can start taking risk corrective measures immediately after the first sprint. Quicker the detection and correction of risk incurring systems or processes, lesser the amount of financial income is at risk, so there is a link to financial benefits as well.

4.2.6 Agility in Operations

The last section of agile business management is dedicated to operations, which refers to all transactional affairs that enable customers to have access to the products and services the company provides. These operations have a variety of subsets, depending on the sector;

- *Manufacturing:* The main operational process of product businesses, to convert the material inputs to customer goods with resources like labor, capital and machineries. The process of manufacturing is dependent on the complexity of the produced good, a car or server manufacturer being the most complex, toward a least complex like dried fruit or ice producer. The priority of manufacturing processes is to fasten the production circle, maintain and increase quality management and optimize the cost of production.
- *Supply Chain*: Includes all outbound logistics of a company's delivery chain. Valid for all product delivery companies, it applies to sectors like the FMCG, e-commerce or pharma. The departmental structure may involve insourced or outsourced logistics and warehouse functions as well. The main focus is optimization of supply chain processes to provide the shortest delivery time, optimized planning and minimized resources.
- *After-Sales Services:* Refers to all transactions a company performs after the product or service is delivered. If the company serves products, the after-sales is related to repair or maintenance of the purchased goods, a common example is electronics for repair or a furniture company for installation. For service companies, the type of service delivered may vary according to the sector, however, claims handling in insurance and loan processing in banking are common examples. Whichever the type, two main priorities for after-sales are to differentiate the service provided to the customer among the close competitors and at the same time minimize the cost of servicing.
- *Contact Center:* The contact center is the only type of operations that apply to 100% of the companies. It can vary from a tire repairer appointment line to a multinational telecommunication company's service line. The main aim of contact center management is to reduce the workforce via chatbot technologies while maximizing the service quality.

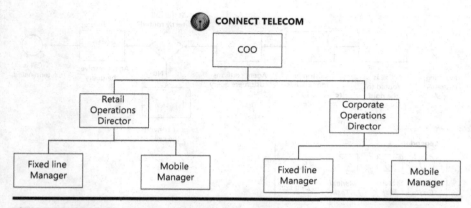

Figure 4.53 A sample telecommunications company management structure.

Regardless of the sector or the type of business, the operational processes play an integral role in the company business management. Furthermore, in the last years, the fierce competition about products and services force companies to deliver a differentiated value and at the same time optimize the costs [63].

Although each subset of operational activities differs, there is a common denominator among all, which is to deliver optimal service at minimized cost. For simplicity, we will focus on contact center structure and explore how agility changes the way companies operate.

Case: For this section, our case study will be a telecommunications company, named Connect, which operates in both fixed-line and mobile services and their customers are segmented as retail and corporate. Their contact center operations are performed under the COO organization, which reports to the company CEO (Figure 4.53).

4.2.6.1 Workflow Management

Operational success relies on effective workflow management. The workflow can be described as the sequence of coordinated tasks in an organization. The workflow defines how a process will flow in the company, and which roles will be responsible for performing activities related to the relevant task. Although creating the work process documentation is an extensive and time-consuming study, there are multiple benefits of analyzing the workflows; re-engineering the flow and either automation or elimination of low-value activities, or concentrating on the customer experience by fastening or improving the service steps are among them [64] (Figure 4.54).

It includes both manual and system activities and the ratio of systematized actions in the workflow represent the automation level of the process [65]. The manual process steps reflect the segregation of work so declares how the work is

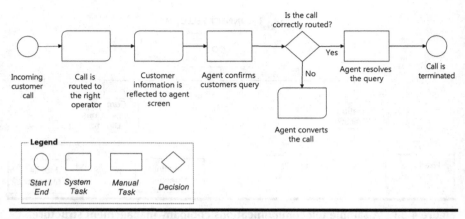

Figure 4.54 A sample incoming call flow in a contact center operations.

organized around the organization. The above-presented sample flow belongs to a contact center where the system tasks and manual tasks are differentiated. The agent, who is taking an active role in the process, belongs to a department in the organization, and his responsibilities are defined by the steps taken in the workflow.

In Connect Telecom, the agent belongs to a fixed-line operations team, under the Retail Operations department. His main responsibilities include responding to retail customer demands and queries about fixed-line issues, resolving customer complaints and offering new promotions to generate sales. His key performance indicators are the number of calls responded, the length of an average call and customer satisfaction level. The managerial responsibilities of this line are to detect process impediments and implement solutions and also to take further improvement actions (Figure 4.55).

Similar agents to this role also exist in other verticals of operations, performing almost identical tasks and also other managerial lines try to manage their work. All might seem fine and in order when you look at the picture as independent units trying to perform their best and it might be the case until things are shaken up with the VUCA effect. Any sort of internal or external change may shake the foundation and affect the operational KPIs of the related department. The effect can be a general system failure of retail fixed-line customers or a newly established regulation that alters the corporate customers' contracts. Whichever the factor, the related unit converts into a crisis mode and employees overtime trying to respond to tripled incoming calls (Figure 4.56).

At that stage, it is not easy for line managers to ask for support from another care center department since their reporting lines and priorities are different and even if the direction comes from the COO (that would be the only way to convince a neighbor department to overtime for you) there is still the open issue that the corporate line unit doesn't know the retail responding screens and processes. The root

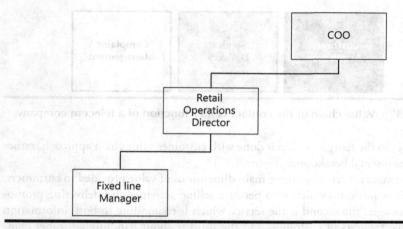

Figure 4.55   A sample telecom company's retail operations structure.

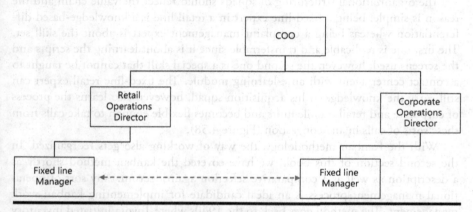

Figure 4.56   A sample telecom company's retail and corporate operations structure.

cause is that these departments were consciously separated and allowed to have different workflows, front ends and even principles.

With no possibility to train the corporate department with retail processes during an ongoing crisis, the only resolution is to overtime and leave a majority of incoming calls dropped on the queue. For customers, not being able to even reach a contact center during an issue is a critical attrition factor.

What happens in agile operational workforce management again starts with the way of organizing: first, the silo structure is changed. The service given should not differentiate whether the caller is a retail or a corporate customer or whether the call is about the fixed or mobile line. The company has a target and ambition to serve the customers in the best and quickest way so things need a shift in the Connect Telecom

Figure 4.57 Value chain of the contact center function of a telecom company.

Company. So the reorganization is done with customer value chain approach, rather than departmental breakdown (Figure 4.57).

The contact centers have three main dimensions of value provided to customers, the first is acquisition, which is to perform selling activities and delivering promotional messages, the second is the service which is responding to both information and service requests of customers and the third is about handling customer complaints with special care and persuading customers not to churn.

The organizational structuring of squads should reflect the value chain and the reason is simple: being a fixed-line expert in a retail line is a knowledge-based differentiation whereas being a complaint management expert is about the skill set. The first one is replicable and transferrable since it is about learning the scripts and the screens used; however, the second one is a special skill that cannot be taught to a contact center agent with an e-learning module. The fixed-line retail expert can still carry the knowledge to his acquisition squad, however, also learns the process of corporate and retail mobile units and becomes flexible enough to take calls from these sorts of calls in any congestion (Figure 4.58).

With the Kanban methodology, the way of working also gets reorganized. In the second section of this book, we have covered the kanban method shortly as a description as well as a comparative selection against scrum. Any sort of operational management process is an ideal candidate for implementing kanban work management. The method goes back to the 1940s where Toyota initiated inventory management, with full transparency of stock levels within the factory floors and communicated the capacity levels between the floors in real time [66].

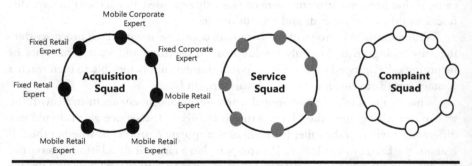

Figure 4.58 Contact center organization based on the value chain.

In today's world, the implication of kanban is matching the workload with the teams' capacity. The teams practicing kanban follow their in and outflow of work, to be able to manage their service levels. In our case, the inflow is the incoming calls and outflow is the service orders or redirected calls to other units, and the worklist includes the active calls.

In order to manage the optimal level of activities, the kanban team needs to visualize their work. The Kanban boards enable this visualization however not every task is displayed like scrum, because in kanban, the number of tasks can easily be 10 times when compared to scrum, so it wouldn't be efficient to track work by manually editing a board. The digital dashboards come to the rescue for teams like contact centers. The department has hung up LCD screens that reflect the amount of work and capacity (Figure 4.59).

The maximum number of calls that can be taken with the whole team being present is called the work in progress limit. The management of the workload would be as expected in ordinary times; however, the external or internal factors creating a jam in the related unit requires instant action taking. If a team overpasses their work in progress limit by a significant degree, which will be visible to all units with the help of the live dashboards, the issue should be handled with urgency [67].

In this working model, the units are not differentiated with the business they serve but according to the value chain. Each member of the contact center knows the screens and scripts of all four business lines. Let's assume due to changing telecommunications regulation, all retail customers are required to renew their fixed-line agreements within 15 days. In the above version, this regulation would end up tripling the number of calls directed to fixed retail line units and was creating a call queue (Figure 4.60).

Assuming that the average call work in progress limit for each unit is three units and at that moment of crisis, the service delivery team faces double the amount of work. Whereas the customer acquisition and the complaint management team both have amounts of work below their usual capacity. This time the calls are under the scope of the service squad and all agents know how to renew a policy of fixed retail line. Without any need for managerial order to support other teams, the customer acquisition starts taking one unit of extra call from the service delivery pool, and

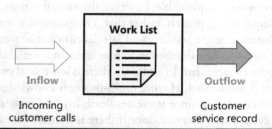

Inflow
Incoming
customer calls

Work List

Outflow
Customer
service record

Figure 4.59 Contact center incoming and outgoing tasks representation.

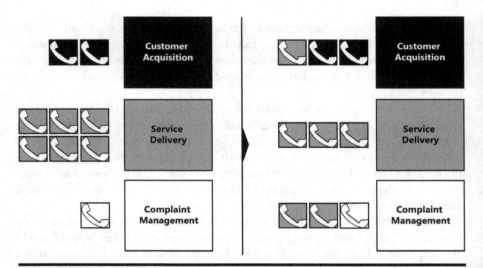

Figure 4.60 Incoming call representation for different contact center units.

the complaint management pulls two units of work. This way the whole workflow is balanced and no customer drops on the line queue.

Benefit: With the value chain organization of your contact center, your priority becomes the customer service. Before the digitalization of work processes, working in a contact center was all about first call resolution and the average length of a call, which made it more about the mechanics. However, with the streamlined contact center processes, correctly routing the customer and eliminating low value-adding calls through chatbot technologies or informative dialing options, the contact center of today is more about the service. With this way of organizing, the right skilled agent can provide the demanded sort of service to the customers.

Another critical benefit is the workflow optimization, which is both linked to service to customers and optimization of resources. As seen in the service delivery hotline issue, the risk of customers falling off the waiting line is the worst outcome a contact center can face. When this happens in a traditional organization, the line manager of the department creates a performance report to the higher management, presenting why the calls couldn't be reached although the whole team overtimed. Surely, the consequence is explainable; however, the negative impact generated is not reversible. In a single unit approach, rather than a fragmented team, only focused on their workload issues generate stability and fair distribution of work.

The fairness in work distribution and cross team support also promotes teamwork and employee engagement. In addition, there is less risk of overtime and churn risk of employees is minimized. Having multi-business knowledge also provides an advantage for the employees since it creates flexibility and favorable career moves. It also shortens cycle time of service since if there is a smaller number of experts in a team, the tasks wait for them and this generates a bottleneck on the process [68].

4.2.6.2 *Continuous Improvement*

All units within an organization have an ongoing duty to repeatedly analyze their workflows and discover improvement opportunities; however, the one unit that is constantly focused on optimization is operations. The main is related to operations departments being perceived as pure cost centers and the outputs being low value. This type of thinking has been forcing the COOs across companies to prioritize cost optimization. The annual target for the COO includes optimizing cost in comparison to the previous year, and the target is a growing one so even if there are substantial changes implemented, the benefits realized become a baseline for the following year's calculation. The managerial staff of an operation department, who automatized orders with direct processing and managed a 10% FTE reduction, gets a higher cost-cutting order for the following year.

What some leaders miss to see in this vicious cycle is that cost reduction going too far in operations represents lower service quality. In order to understand the effect of this, we can deep dive into an example scenario with the same telecom company.

Case: Connect telecom retail department had implemented an automated call routing system for its fixed-line calls, seeing that a majority of service calls in the previous year were adaptable to chatbot. Chatbot adaptability can be measured by repetitive calls, with similar questions and answers. In order to estimate the effect of chatbot, you can pick a sufficient number of service records, analyze the number of repeated records and calculate the effect of converting similar calls to the bot response. In Connect telecom, the analysis shows repetitive calls around customer requests about learning the latest invoice amount of their line in use. Seeing the potential of automation, the retail fixed-line manager agreed on a bot conversion development (Figure 4.61).

The retail fixed line is a service line where there are 10,000 daily incoming calls and 100 agents responding to these calls, making 100 calls per agent a day the

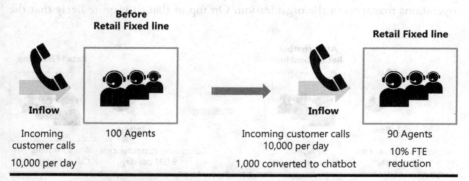

Figure 4.61 Chatbot implementation effect on a sample telecom company's contact center.

average performance of the department. The chatbot project team manages to convert 10% of daily calls to the bot response mechanism and cover the invoice checking demands of customers with no negative effect on customer experience. With the success of the project, the retail fixed-line manager is appreciated within that calendar year. However, facing a higher efficiency target the following year, taking the 10% as a baseline, the CEO and the COO increases the expectations with another 10% reduction target.

Facing a top-down target system, the retail fixed-line manager has no option but to oblige to the additional 10% saving. Since after implementation of chatbot, there is less room for optimization and since any further infrastructural improvements take more than a calendar year, the manager decides to cut the number of agents directly by 10%, dropping nine more as a last resort (Figure 4.62).

Since the additional cut of resources is not an optimization outcome, this means the same number of incoming calls, 9,000 per day/agent in this case, are continuing to inflow and the average capacity to respond to calls per agent is still 100. With the same capacity and 81 agents, 81*100=8,100 calls would be responded with regular service levels, which means 900 calls per day will be dropped. (A dropped or lost call means a customer hanging up before reaching a contact center agent.) As mentioned above, the dropped calls ratio is one of the red flags in a contact center organization [69].

A second type of issue with the standard way of implementing improvement opportunities is that the tactical or architectural optimization actions are both planned and executed based on the sub-department requirements. To put it more clearly, going back to the Connect Telecom company, the chatbot technology, which is leveraged to eliminate low service value calls, is a specific implementation to the retail fixed line. The root cause is simple: the organizational model as well as the KPI targets are linked to the fragmented structure, so the fixed retail line manager facing target pressure to optimize calls initiates an IT task to implement chatbot. The technology is a definite priority (in some tough work environments, these top-down targets can even mean a matter of existence for the manager) for the fixed retail line manager and it may not be a priority or may not even cross the minds of other three operations managers in the organization. On top of that, it is quite likely that the

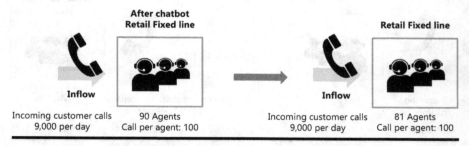

Figure 4.62 FTE effect of chatbot implementation on a sample telecom company's contact center department.

fixed retail line manager does not feel the obligation to discuss the need beforehand with her peers and in the rest of the cases. Even if she takes proactive initiative to share and invite other managers to her project, it may not draw sufficient attention from the others. However, we all know that once the benefits of the deployed solution are in place, the other departments start asking about it and try to replicate the solution for their own processes as well. Another likely scenario which is even more problematic is that the corporate segment simultaneously trying to implement a similar solution, with a different vendor independently. The second scenario is more troubled since the duplication of efforts and systems result in unnecessary cost burden to all. Basically, whichever the case, they signal misalignment and inefficiency of internal governance.

In agile approach, continuous improvement is not a separate effort but closely tied to the ongoing work. The philosophy of this approach is driven by lean principles of Six Sigma Methodology: the method explained by Salah et al. as a disciplined and structured approach is used to enhance process performance [70]. This method includes many principles that can be applied within the organizations and application of kanban or scrumban. Teams using a workflow system can visualize necessary information to prioritize and pull work from the work pool as well as transparently visualize the impediments of the process and reflect improvement opportunities [71].

The most practical way to implement the visualization would enable instant detection of impediments or roadblocks is a board with a swim lane. The common board includes three simple classifications of work based on the status, which is to do, progress and done. There are more detailed versions you may come up with including other sub-statuses like review or tests. However, in summary, the blocks are about the status of the relevant task, user story, where a separate post is dedicated to each story (Figure 4.63).

What comes as an improved version of kanban is the scrumban board, with the inclusion of the swim lanes, where the work is differentiated by daily and ongoing activities that are foundation to the department's work, which are called "run" activities. In our example workflow, taking a call or recording the call outcome or opening a complaint ticket can be considered as run actions. Another swim lane is dedicated to the work in progress limit notion, as we have covered in the above section of this chapter. The work that comes as an inflow, which is beyond the relevant team's standard capacity is considered as above WIP limit. It is highly beneficial to visualize these types of activities since they are the ultimate candidate for the next section.

The change swim lane refers to the user stories that will be generated based on the issues identified on the upper lanes. A candidate story in change lane can be about chatbot implementation due to blocked calls or changing the record entry screens of agents to a more user-friendly version, it can also be an innovation workshop of the team, which is planned to generate new ideas for out-of-box solutions.

To further systematize this flow, it would be useful to mix change agents in the squads. If the squad includes members out of the daily operations, to manage

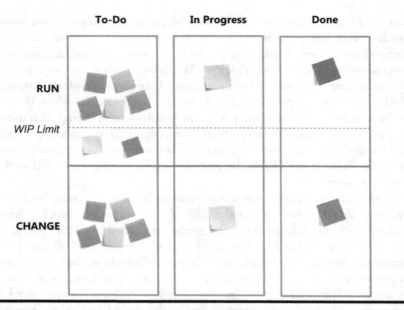

Figure 4.63   A sample Kanban board, displaying WIP limit.

change activities, then the team converts from applying kanban to scrumban. The relevant expertise can be a system analyst role, which is a blended responsibility of a developer and business analyst, who works actively with the team. He does not take operational tasks from the inflow but he defines his own backlog, based on the agile routines of the team. Also, the co-location principle applies so the analyst works together with the team. He attends the ceremonies and explores new optimization opportunities (Figure 4.64).

The team can be extended further with other relevant members of teams. Since we have covered the risk and compliance attendance for lines of defenses, a risk expert would be valid to continuously assess the ongoing risks and take risk eliminating backlog items (Figure 4.65).

The delivery of these types of improvement tasks is possible with the relevant members of the squad coming together. When the team agrees on a common user story, the related expert role becomes the default owner of the story and adds other members (either by voluntary principle or based on specific expertise) to their tasks (Figure 4.66).

First, the user story is created, stating the stakeholder, the task and the goal. The story is coded and located on the board. In the illustrated example, the requirement detected by the service squad is a system development which enables an agent to instantly screen all recent records that were recorded from the same customer. The benefit of the task is that the agent will not waste time looking for older records

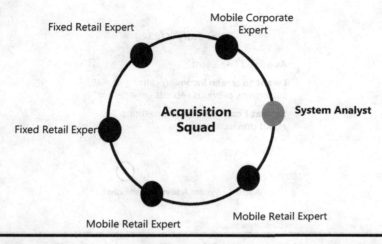

Figure 4.64 A sample agile organizational model for contact center operations.

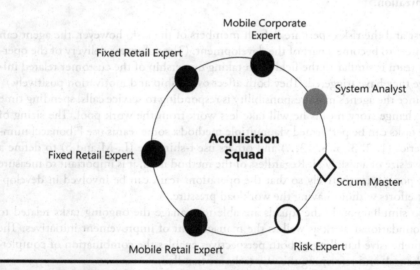

Figure 4.65 A sample agile organizational model for contact center operations, including cross functional support.

if the customer on the call is referring to a previous service that she did with the contact center.

Below the story, the teaming is also represented. This step is to define who within the squad is working on this story. In our example, the system analyst performs the development of the front end that automatically generates the call summary, the risk expert defines which customer data is compliant to be visible to the agent and the agent himself to design the best end-user experience. As mentioned, the system

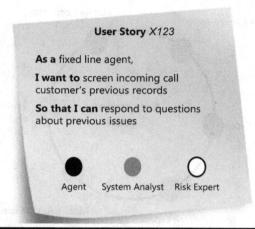

Figure 4.66 A sample user story of the service squad, in an agile contact center organization.

analyst and the risk expert are default members of the task; however, the agent can volunteer to become a part of the development. (The volunteer delivery of the operation team is similar to the field team taking ownership of the customer related initiative they have triggered. They both affect ownership and motivation positively.)

Since the agent's main responsibility is responding to service calls, spending time on a change story means he will take less work from the work pool. The sizing of these tasks can be performed via multiple methods: some teams use Fibonacci number series (1, 2, 3, 5, 8, 13...) and others use t-shirt size (L, M and S) to define a relative size of a task [72]. Regardless of the method used, it is important to measure work pools quantitatively so that the operations team can be involved in development efforts without having the workload pressure.

So simultaneously the squads are able to manage the ongoing tasks related to the foundational work as well as the management of improvement initiatives. The comprehensive handling of both perspectives enables the combination of completing the task and reforming the way tasks are handled.

Benefits: The major benefit of this approach is the scale of improvement opportunities when compared to standard management of operation optimization. First of all, the efforts of implementing initiatives, which used to be separate, are merged and aligned. This leads to magnifying the expected gains, simultaneously to multiple departments, where the development effort is applicable. As we have seen in the chatbot example, not only the fixed retail line but also all other business lines start benefiting from the efficiency of the new technology instantly.

Another realized difference is the runners and the changers becoming a part of the same team. When a system designer or a risk expert is independent of the team running the tasks, they might not have full visibility of the internal bottleneck.

As a result, the offered solutions from these units do not completely fit the operation team's necessities. A system analyst, who delivers a screen design for an agent's usage, on the basis of a description written by the agent, may not fulfill the optimal flow.

In addition, these stakeholders miss the opportunities to proactively generate development opportunities. A risk expert's outside in evaluation, in regards to the operational flow or data entry system helps him to detect possibilities that might converge to risk and take proactive actions.

Whichever model is applied, there is efficiency gain. Although the concept of efficiency can be strongly perceived as a number of employee calculations, it applies to a wider concept, including training, reduced errors or shortened lag time.

Finally, the operational units in transformed organizations start to be considered as service centers rather than cost centers. The previous negative effect of extensive cost cutting can be better managed and the service quality can be kept at optimum.

Chapter 5

Agile Enablers

In the last section, I try to cover the tools and methodologies that enable an easier, smoother and more successful agile transformation for a corporation. These notes are based on a couple of years of transformational experience, the lessons learned, the mistakes and regrets. So I hope it would be a guideline for starters or implementers within this area.

The enterprise agility transformation in a scale described in this book, where all business units adapt to their people, roles, processes, technologies and mindset is not like any other transition private companies have ever faced. All common transformational themes of the last 20 to 30 years were around a domain, an area of expertise. For instance, in the late 1990s and in the beginning 2000s the most popular trend was about centralization and outsourcing. Companies with fragmented operations, throughout a country or globally, started to centralize their organization's certain expertise in low-cost locations. The most common example of this approach was contact center and software development team unification overseas. It was a trend that spread most rapidly due to the benefits promised, incredible cost efficiency: soon an accountant of a multinational in Austria was calling her human resources business partner to ask about an item in her payroll summary, and suddenly the call was diverted to an Indian colleague who had to call back to check Austrian payroll system. So the benefits of these were later highly questioned. In any case, within this transformation type, the human resources and operations domains were the most affected parties, and the rest of the organization realized the change when their local line dial was automatically converted overseas.

Then in the mid-2000s, the customer-oriented organization wave hit the organizations around the world. The most common profiles affected by this movement were multinationals with a product mindset, who also offer services, so the logical forerunners were banks, insurance companies and telecommunication companies. The main concentration was maximizing customer satisfaction in the end-to-end journey as also explained in the agility in the marketing chapter. The main parties involved in the transformation effort were marketing and sales.

Just the following decade and I may say still ongoing was dedicated to digital transformation. All efforts were united to convert the companies' both internal process and the customer-facing interfaces to digital. As it is linked to the previous trend, the digitization activities that would directly affect the customer experience were prioritized. All the internal digitization efforts were concentrated on the cost saving automation initiatives, as explained in agility in operations. So that both the top line and bottom line were positively affected. The parties within the company to be affected by digital transformation were information technologies, marketing and operations.

The commonality of all these different sorts of change efforts was that on the one side, they didn't shake the core of the organization whatever the scale of implementation was. On the other side, the enterprise agility transformation leaves no stone unturned, meaning no part of the company continues their work as designed 20 years ago or no process is left unquestioned in that sense. So as a comparison to other common change waves in the corporate world, the scale of enterprise agility is quite exponential.

This magnitude of change requires much more than the traditional approach to change management. Change management is in fact a theme that became a trend during this mass transformation period of the last 30 years. It simply refers to the activities implemented in order to ease and fasten adaptation of a company to the changing environment. When organizations started to apply these common trends like digitalization, centralization or customer orientation, the league of consultants, including me at that time, came in and suggested the approach of change management. Almost all large corporations have built Change Management Departments dedicated to these efforts. It involved mainly internal and external communication efforts and some human resources initiatives, like printing coffee cups with the logo of transformation and distributing them to the project teams or organizing town halls with leaders so that they can talk about how beneficial the change will be. The changes were more system oriented and only engaged attention of certain parts of the organization. And even if none of these efforts were applied, the employees would find their way through by asking a colleague or two, figuring out how the system works finally.

With agility, the change management had to take its position and actions to the next level. The change plan had to be long term, I would say two years in minimum for a firm with 500+ employees, the scope had to be not certain groups of teams but the whole set of employees, and finally the depth of the touch had to be deeper, just superficial kickoff cocktails would not be sufficient. In this section, I try to explain the sorts of actions that can be taken to give that depth so that the whole company internalizes the change.

5.1 Culture

I choose to start with the toughest topic under change agenda: the culture. But I have to declare that it is not a sub-topic but rather an encompassing one and whatever action is executed in the other sub-topics serves culture primarily. So it is useful to approach the concept collectively. I prefer not to go deep into the psychological aspects of corporate life and the meaning of culture in depth and rather suggest the best reading for agile culture which is Reinventing Organizations by Frederic Laloux [73]. I highly value his work in terms of simplifying such a complex topic as culture by simply color coding the organizational models and reflecting the evolution of those models through time.

In that model, the historical evolution of all sorts of organizations is plotted. The ancient one, the red organization, refers to fear led organizations like gangs where there is submission to the ultimate leader. There are no rules or processes to control the system. The red is followed by amber, the ultimate leader is replaced by hierarchy and is followed by rules, not chaos as red brings. Typical example being the military system where the rules secure the application of military standards. The green on the other hand is completely the opposite, family-like structures like the non-governmental organizations, communities, who have no leaders, praise engagement above all.

Beyond all, what draws my attention is the orange organization that summarizes the private corporations' working model, acting like a big machine with connected wheels, where the oil that turns the wheels is the profit [73]. Making more profit is the main driver of the organization, and this is ensured by strictly applied hierarchy, the top-down objectives these leaders push toward the employees and the control processes that ensure that the objectives are met. Achieving the top-down targets is the sole communicated purpose which creates an enormous level of competition among employees as well as other players in the market. The concept of value generation is accepted as money generation, and this is accomplished with less consideration of corporate values, employee engagement, customer satisfaction and so on. It's not a coincidence that typical leaders who easily climb the career ladder among these companies have the common prototype: reckless and fearless, who feels no regrets taking actions at the expense of others, who leads by pushing ideas and deadlines.

Another drawback is as explained in organizational agility, the top-down order concept leaves no space for attachment to a higher purpose and creativity among employees. They don't find or discover what to do but rather tell what to do.

We can easily claim that the orange type includes all companies since the industrial revolution and has minimally challenged until the agile transformation brought an opportunity for a new culture. In other words, with every part of the operating model evolving through decades, the orange model was the only concept that survived and is still ongoing in the majority of the organizations. Since the orange culture is not applicable to the agility concept, a new definition was required.

The introduced cultural classification by Laloux is the Teal organization. The main driver of the organization strictly shifts from monetary gains toward purpose.

The shift also underlines the metaphor change of machines to living organisms and starts working as a united and complex system [74]. How this is accomplished is about all the previous sections in this book, but "why it matters" is summarized by Laloux into three philosophies: self-management, wholeness and evolutionary purpose.

All three principles work together to create the atmosphere that is most creative. We have covered the concept of breaking the long-lasted walls of organizational hierarchy in sufficient longitude in the organizational agility chapter. Self-management brings autonomy, autonomy creates freedom of thinking and freedom of thinking triggers breakthrough [75]. The breakthrough may be related to the person, more like self-actualization, to achieve the lifelong purpose, the İkigai in some cases [76]. When wholesomeness is introduced with purpose, the breakthrough is about the work mission, it's about elevating the team you are working together with. The mission can be finding a new molecule for a rare type of cancer or about shortening delivery time with a supply chain optimization module you code, no matter how big or small, it is about giving work satisfaction to you and the people you work with.

5.2 Mindset

In order for the culture to disseminate toward the core, the mindset needs to shift as well. Easier said than done, this one is crucial to shape the culture and equally difficult to change. Although there are dozens of social psychology research on the manner, I am not an expert and I prefer approaching the mindset topic from a more tangible angle, as below:

First of all, when we say agile mindset, there are a couple of favored behaviors that are praised.

- *Service oriented:* As explained in agility in marketing, the organizations continuously put the customer in the center of their design. This requires employees who design the customer services to have a service-oriented mindset. This mindset is about shifting thinking toward the customer's needs and thinking as if in their shoes. These behaviors underline a character with empathy. A person with empathetic behavior can easily think and act with the need of another and would be able to reflect the thinking to actions.
- *Enterprise thinker:* This one is closely related to wholesomeness and it is fairly simple if the team I am working on is generating wonderful results and another neighbor team in my company is suffering a work crisis and spending plus five hours on average in the office, me leaving the office at 5 pm can be understandable in an orange environment but not in teal. The enterprise thinker is someone who puts the whole company's benefits forward. Before taking any action about an initiative, the enterprise thinker scans around the environment and involves other business units or parties who might benefit from that initiative, actively shares and scales the benefit to be created. The reciprocity

of this behavior among the whole environment connects the person to the company on a deeper level.

■ *Innovative:* Innovation is not invention as commonly confused so what I want to emphasize with this behavior is certainly not an inventive capability but rather an ability to think differently, think outside the box. Someone with an eagerness to explore new ideas, not to take things for granted would perform greatly in an agile team. In an agile team with no innovators, the sprint planning ceremony simply becomes a to-do list generation with every member of the team one by one declaring what it is they were supposed to do in that calendar week(s) and score the work. However, planning with innovators is a joyful activity to be a part of, where the excited minds gather around a table to tackle the customer issues with new approaches, bringing out of nowhere ideas to the sprint backlog.

■ *Experimental:* I link this behavior with courageousness since it is about finding new ways to do the tasks that have been well learnt through the years. Experimentalism is related to innovative thinking, however, two concepts are independent. The idea can be new and the implementation can be experimental or the task is a repetitive one; however, the experimental approaches the same task with a completely new vision. It is also about risk awareness because when there is a completely new work concept, a product to be launched for the first time only digitally, for instance, experimenting always supports minimizing the risk with a smaller audience, observing the errors or flaws in the process and acting instantly for correction.

■ *Growth oriented:* Having a growth mindset comes to life in two ways, one is for the person's own being, which is to add new skills and capabilities to themselves in order to grow in their career or life (which was covered in detail in agility in human resources – career architecture section) or to act proactively to support the growth of the environment, the team, the department they belong to. The second one is about business agility and each member of the team aiming for collective growth. This can only happen if individuals in the team have growth mindset, in other words are disturbed by routine tasks, do not get satisfied with a business revenue similar to the last five years.

This sort of mindset is long believed to be tackled with change management techniques; which are stated primarily as two tactical sets of activities: training and communication. Transformation offices all around the world find communicating the new culture and training the employees with the new culture would be sufficient; however, I can tell from my experience that there is no impulse – response logic behind mindset. The people who have worked in a traditional organization for 20 years do not start acting with wholesomeness after a three-day training camp in a fancy hotel room nor do they after receiving communication newsletters involving CEO speech about new ways of working. It is unfortunately much more complex and effort taking than that. I of course do not claim these efforts are meaningless, they certainly set the stage for the new tone of internal communication and enable transparently sharing the strategy.

What becomes important is the steps taken after the communication, the launch event and training are completed, which is the internalization. For people with the right mindset, or some call "born agile", the adoption is straightforward, the change of the tone comes instantly and most importantly, naturally. Those employees start applying principles themselves so they are the easy targets; however, unfortunately they are also the minority.

At this point, I would also like to rule out the individuals who have unwillingness about any change in the company, who have very low levels of engagement for a certain period of time, however, due to personal circumstances still continue to work for that company. I find them almost impossible to change (Figure 5.1).

For the rest, which can be considered as targeted segments, the approach needs to be more systematic. The environment the employees experience needs to shift so that even if they are not born with those behaviors they can still learn them. So figuratively we should aim for the middle segment of employees, who claim the majority in terms of number and who have a possibility to shift mindset.

For the middle segment, the most effective method is creating new practices, new environments that the employees are motivated to think differently but are not forced to act differently. All the practices we have covered in people and culture are good examples of forces helping the mindset shift. A couple of examples would I think help to clarify.

Case: A large company I worked with had an organization chart published to the whole company with a structure that emphasized hierarchy, there were multiple layers in the organization and the chart had different colors of each layer, within each box the titles were written in bold, it was republished whenever there is an organizational change, so the message of status was redelivered continuously. Of course, leaving hierarchy behind is a long process, but there was one action we have implemented that was simple enough to start thinking differently. We had removed all the color codes in the boxes and also removed the titles within the boxes (Figure 5.2).

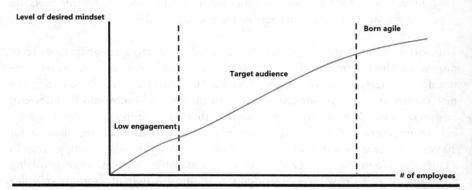

Figure 5.1   Shift of mindset curve.

To represent this to the Retail Operations Director was complicated; if "Retail Operations" they saw differently in display. Identifying the structure on the Director, specifying to the level, someone who needs to reach the retail operations department across. I now understood; without giving importance to this, ... is not a valid mechanism since their respective hierarchical boundaries or indications it was fine used for an additional functional status.

... multiple words of these retail elements is the way to a better culture to ... imitate ... There is like simpler of small example but the message is the same ... to know the new business meetings, with modified layers an environment ... where people can change, and can adapt to an agile network.

5.5 Leadership

The final topic is leadership, a logical consequence of the list, two, in any sort of agile enablers for ... an organizational or enterprise, or even process-level leadership. Due to a more specific ... ... acquiring of transformation, their influence is more evident. The main reason is the overall change, or the shifting the concept of autonomy to the team, this has an impact ... it is in different terms, it is deciding what the ... developing ... the transformation process in to operating, it is how it is the discretionary functions, also deciding within a role in organizational agility and in enterprise culture, it is ... ... (Figure 5.3).

Do you wonder ... As simply ... ... the last piece of leadership transformation is the agility, where the responsibility of a project in terms of delivery and over the timeline becomes ... ... with ... people service becomes the application over the team, that translates the decision-making for every ...

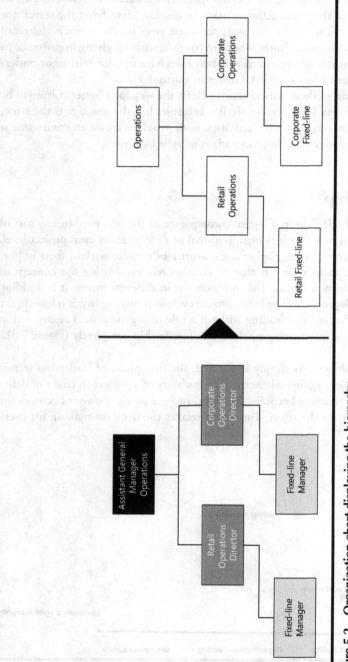

Figure 5.2 Organization chart displaying the hierarchy.

So, as presented in the figure, the Retail Operations Director was communicated as Retail Operations, there was differentiation in display, identifying the status nor the "Director" specification. In this way, someone who needs to reach the retail operations department would know whom to contact, without giving importance to the title or status within the organization. Their roles have not diminished or underrated; it was just freed from additional forces of status.

So multiplication of these critical actions clears the way for a better culture to be internalized. There may be dozens of similar examples but the message is the same, try to introduce new concepts with activities, with proof, to create an environment where people can change their habits to adapt to agile behaviors.

5.3 Leadership

The third topic is leadership in a logical consequence of the first two. In any sort of agile transformation, whether it is organizational or enterprise, or even project level, leadership plays a crucial role. Higher the maturity of transformation, their importance doubles. The main reason is that all changes rely on shifting the concept of autonomy to the delivery teams. This autonomy is in different forms: it is deciding what the next development will be in the project cycle in project agility, it is leaving the director approach behind and leading without a title in organizational agility and in enterprise agility, it is about changing the style of leadership completely (Figure 5.3).

■ *Decision autonomy*: As simply illustrated, the first phase of leadership transition is in project agility, where the responsibility of a project in terms of delivery, cost and timeline becomes the team, and the product owner becomes the spokesperson for the team. The leader relaxes the decision-making for every

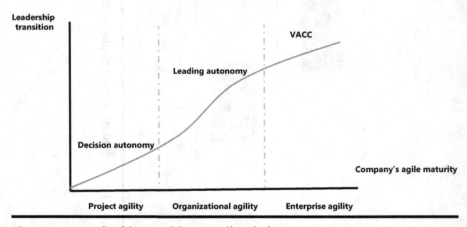

Figure 5.3   Leadership transition to agile mindset.

design detail and follows the team outcomes via sprint reviews, giving feedback for future actions. The leader is transformed into a sponsor at this stage, still has the organizational status or titles that the corporation gives so there is a logical continuation of traditional leadership.

■ *Leading autonomy*: In the second level of maturity, where the organizational agility is in place, the leader delegates simply the leading autonomy. There is a product owner who is not only responsible but also accountable for the business actions planned and executed. The squad members do not report to this product owner, so there is no shift of autonomy. Although the first one is also controversial, this level can (and does) create a serious level of anxiety. Especially when the new cultural thinking is not internalized across the company, the leaders enter a self-questioning state of mind. In order to manage this anxiety, preparing the existing people leaders for what is to come and how they can bring the most value to the team is most critical. P&C members are expected to take an active role in this transition.

■ *VACC*: The last and final stage of leadership transformation in the agile universe represents a shift in the description of the leadership. It is a bigger magnitude of change, however, easier to embrace when compared to the second stage of change. The reason is that as well as dropping some behaviors like planning, directing and controlling, at this stage the leader takes on different sets of responsibilities. So the acceptance is easier, however, adoption to a new skill set is tougher.

  – *V of VACC is visionary*: the responsibility to draw attention to a compelling common purpose within the organization.

  – *A of VACC is architect*: the second responsibility is to replace the top-down planner hat, and rather bring together the team and design the high-level system, which serves the vision stated. By setting the business architecture well, the leader enables the product teams to follow the path.

  – *C of VACC is coach*: since the teams will take on the responsibility of delivering the business, the leader concentrates on coaching the members, so that they find their way through. The coaching can be related to the person's skill set, the approach taken to succeed or functional expertise. Within coaching, the leader can either directly respond to those needs or, when necessary, guide the coachee to the right place to get support.

  – *C of VACC is a catalyst*: as a catalyst, the leader acts as a bridge within the company, to bring together the right people who would be able to deliver the promised outcome and remove their obstacles to fasten the implementation of the tasks. They are the enabler of wholesomeness, by creating a secure, transparent and energetic space where people will be willing to deliver their best together [77].

So the one-dimensional role becomes four-dimensional and requires to include a new set of capabilities. As explained when the difference of cultures was stated, the leaders in traditional companies have a lot of unlearning responsibilities to adapt to. Those leaders learnt how to be a directing leader watching and copying their executives, as those executives who learned similarly. This becomes like a chronic disease as the gene is passed from generation to generation. As a result, implanting the model in the 21st century is a serious obstacle. Through this transformation journey, it is possible to face leaders who are lost causes, as well as born agile leaders.

Case: I experienced a transformation in a large organization where two Assistant General Managers in the company were converting to the VACC. As a logical initial step, we applied the right training and coaching to those leaders. The first one was a lost cause where the other was a natural born. The first one asked to approve every single decision taken in the team and became frustrated in case of missing a meeting or discussion. While another one who was located in a corner office, with a huge desk and a special sitting area, gave back his desk and area, ordered a usual size working desk and asked it to be placed right in the middle of the team he was working with. This happened on the first day of agile transformation, where everyone stepped into the newly established office floor for squads, they saw their leader greeting them in the middle of the office floor. One action, one day and the sense of the wholeness spread as fast as current.

So the mission of company general managers is to evaluate the existing leaders in the organization and assess either internally or externally, whether they are a lost cause or natural-born VACC. After that analysis, it is wise for the top management to reassign leaders that are eligible to the new culture if the company is seriously considering applying enterprise agility. All the business or customer or employee related benefits we have covered in agility in the business section comes with a prize, and the prize is to be able to let go of toxic profiles who drag the organization backward.

It is obvious that if you desire cultural transformation within the company, the change has to start from the top leadership. When the leaders act as role models and they take actions against their status or hierarchy, the rest of the employees follow.

5.4 Coaching

We have covered that for this middle segment of employees and leaders who aim to be transformed via a dedicated change management program, won't take only days. As the training and communications last almost a week in most cases, the rest is in the hands of change agents within the organization. These agents have the responsibility to ensure that the new ways of working are always on track, and the culture is progressing in the right direction. They work and breathe with the agile teams, observe their work and attitudes closely and have the ability to intervene whenever they find necessary.

These agents can be assigned in two models, one is dedicated, which are fewer in number and transforming the culture is their sole responsibility, and the second is the voluntary model. We will come back to the first group in detail, but I want to explain the second group first. Larger the organization, it would not be sustainable to assign dedicated people all around the company to spend full time with the agile teams, especially when it is at the enterprise level. So instead the companies can assign change agents among the organization as an additional responsibility. These people volunteer to take on the job; however, they should be evaluated whether they carry the right mindset. Later, they continue delivering their usual duties in their department, where they bring new approaches or support to the teams they belong to as a role model. In order to apply this model, the transformation office needs to keep close distance and support the change agents with relevant methodologies. The acceptance of this approach among the company members is generally high since the positive change messages come from their colleagues, not only from leaders or P&C.

The dedicated support to agile teams also comes in two ways, with scrum masters and agile coaches. We briefly described the roles in the organizational agility chapter but it would be useful to give further detail about the importance of their contribution.

5.4.1 Scrum Master

In project agility, the scrum master is a usual member of the squad, who is a profile capable of resolving issues and has good communication skills, the scrum master responsibilities come on top of his work and in many cases the teams rotate the scrum master to balance the additional work caused by the responsibility. In this phase, there is application and assignment to the role, no evaluation of whether the person who has the scrum master hat has the required skill set to perform the tasks well.

In enterprise agility, the scrum master is the member of the team and is dedicated to ensure that the agile practices are performed well. Their sole responsibility is scrum mastering and handling a couple of squads depending on the sizing. They attend all ceremonies of the squad and work on removing any sort of impediment within the business or teaming. They also run the retrospective ceremonies by applying different liberating structures to question whether the team achieved their sprint goal and if not, what root causes hindered their journey. They allow the unspeakable truths about the team performance to be discussed so that corrective actions can be taken. Since squads have a work backlog, the scrum master has a retrospective related backlog on the side, so that he can work on the team impediments offline, one by one.

An enabler for the scrum master is measuring the agile maturity of the squad periodically and concentrating on the areas where the team falls behind. The agile maturity model has a questionnaire related to the structure (whether the ceremonies are applied well, whether the team is creating MVPs, whether the planning sessions are created with design thinking approach etc.), related to governance (whether there is a work alignment in between other related teams, whether there is transparency and efficient workflow, whether the key stakeholders are a part of the sprint reviews etc.) and finally related to the mindset (whether every team member is innovative, whether the team has a feeling of common purpose, whether workload is fair among the members). The results of the assessment shed light on which area the scrum master should concentrate on in the upcoming terms.

5.4.2 Agile Coach

The agile coach acts as an advocate of agile mindset and processes throughout the organization. The difference of project agility versus enterprise agility is less when compared to the scrum master role since the agile coach has to be fewer in number and be completely dedicated to the teams they are responsible for. The main goal of the agile coach is to manage the rhythm of the agile governance in the organization and take actions toward increasing adaptation.

Unlike the scrum master, the agile coach doesn't need to be involved in each and every daily stand up of squads but needs to have a general understanding of where the squads stand in terms of structure, governance and mindset. So they work closely with the tribe or squad level scrum masters, frequently review their evaluation of the agile maturity index and suggest corrective or preventive activities. The direct responsibility of the agile coach is to act when they see an overarching theme around all squads, which resembles a company level impediment. Then they plan more collective actions to resolve the issues. For instance, if not one but almost all squads cannot comprehend how to apply the design thinking methodology, they can plan a companywide workshop to teach and remind the importance of design thinking for getting the customer's insight.

They are also responsible for synchronization among squads/tribes which is also another important process. It is rather ironic that the squads, which are formed to fight back the silo structure that used to put a certain distance between the departments, are from time to time creating "new silos" among themselves. The synchronization ceremonies, which are shortly called the syncs, are about gathering the squads or tribes to discuss the key business priorities and agree on common actions. The enterprise coach builds these sorts of gatherings and chairs them.

The third responsibility is to handle the leadership team's ceremony requirements; the executive committee should convert to reflect the VACC behaviors as well as bottom-up strategy building. So the agile coach facilitates executive committees to enable the new way of working to be applied at the leadership level. This is an important mission since adaptability at leadership ease adoption of the rest of the organization.

The proactive actions of the coach are not limited to the team level or enterprise-level activities. As the name also implies, the coach is expected to deliver agile coaching to critical members. They listen to the worries and constraints and tries to understand what can be done at the cultural level to better internalize the change. So as an overall, the duty of the agile coach is highly critical in the transformation road map.

5.5 Strategy

The next enabler is the way strategy is planned, circulated and executed. How the strategic plan is formed is very critical in terms of defining what the enterprise will focus on and how it will work. If it is done right, it can act as an enabler for shifting mindsets.

It is well known that the traditional leadership acts as a definer of the strategy and not only defines the top level but also goes deeper into the sub-categories, and in some cases with highly controller profiles, even the tasks are planned and directed to their teams. In majority, the board comes together for a strategic workshop, 2–3 days offsite, discuss what the priority is for the company, set certain outcomes to be achieved through the year and let the communications department circulate them through the organization. The C level leaders going out of this strategy camp, goes back to their direct reports and orders the outcomes to be achieved. The rest is a cascade down story we all know very well. Those outcomes also become the balanced scorecard of the departments and are managed as the KPIs, as explained in the agility in the finance section of this book (Figure 5.4).

There are more than one issues related to this flow, but the main points are:

■ *Lack of insight*: The leadership builds the strategy with what they have in mind or what they have read about in a popular business magazine, or in some cases, what a group of consultants have presented to them. As a result, the insight of customers, business partners and employees are unfortunately not taken into account. The proposed subset of activities might not be wrong or false; however, they are often not the primary needs of the customer.

■ *Authority bias*: The board exiting the strategy camp coming with orders have definitely less room for adapting and improving, what they have planned has to be achieved and the people listening cannot and do not question or reject what is being told. Avinash Kaushik calls this dilemma, the highest-paid person's opinion, HIPPO, it is about the rigidity of the leader's opinion when approaching a new strategy or concept [78]. If the HIPPO effect takes place

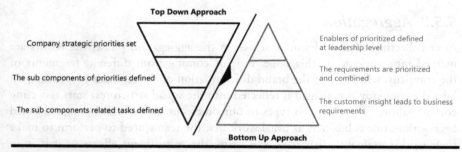

Figure 5.4   Top down vs bottom up strategy.

in a strictly bureaucratic organization, the rest of the team is easily silenced, and the risk of accepting a wrong idea grows.

■ *Internalization*: The third issue comes as a consequence of the first two points, the lack of internalization of the company strategy. An employee engagement survey conducted by Deloitte in 2019 stated that 73% of the employees responded by saying internalization of the purpose of the company affects their engagement with the company positively [79]. Considering the direction is driven from the purpose but coming from the scrambled notes of the C level out of the strategy meeting, there is less chance for the receiving end to be able to internalize.

The agile way of strategic planning is completely different from the accustomed way. First and foremost the top-down strategy no longer exists, and all strategic planning depends heavily on what the business teams prioritize. The flow of strategy creation is also completely reversed.

5.5.1 Insight Gathering

As a primary step, the insight teams gather all the inputs from three main sources: the customer, the stakeholders and the employees. This is a comprehensive process so should be planned prior to the strategic planning cycle. The customer insight can come from multiple sources, like contact center satisfaction reports, brand-level market research and social media comments related to the company's products and services. The stakeholder insight is a topic that is usually overlooked; however, it plays a critical role in truly understanding the company perception within the network of players. So the business partners are interviewed: they are usually the buyers, the supply chain companies, the firms which some company processes are outsourced to like warehouse management. What they will tell about the company will be crucial for shedding light on areas of improvement. Last but not least is what the employees think about the company position, in terms of responding to their own demands as well as responding to their customer's needs.

5.5.2 Aggregation

After collecting all the relevant insights, in the aggregation phase, the results are merged into buckets. At this stage, insights coming from different fragments of the company, whether it is the brand differentiation or the segment (depending on how the company is managed is reflected into the squad structures) start reflecting commonalities. There are two types of outcomes out of the brand or squad-based aggregation: one is business as usual work that the teams need to perform to make their work sustainable, if it is an HR team, the recruitment efforts or if it is an IT department the software development coding is called foundation work. What

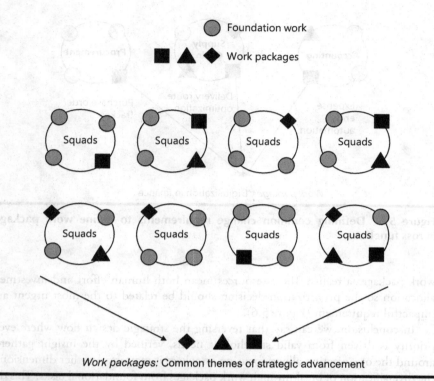

Figure 5.5 Foundational vs exponential work differentiation.

comes beyond the work requirements that are defined to improve or reshape the departmental work are called the work packages (Figure 5.5).

Not surprisingly, the work packages of squads underline similar business requirements, and the answers to those requirements are also complementary. An example of this flow can be the finance department with independent squads named, accounting, procurement and supply chain. Although they are managed under the same roof, their foundational work is quite differentiated, expense entry to delivery report to purchasing order gathering. However, they might have the work packages of delivery chain route optimization to accounting entry automation, which all highlight the need for digitalization.

5.5.3 Prioritization

At the last stage, the combined and aggregated themes reach the board level for prioritization. The example used in the aggregation phase is valid, the common theme of supply chain, procurement and accounting is to invest in digital technologies to improve the efficiency and quality of finance. As a result, the CFO agrees and prioritizes the digital change portfolio and allocates sufficient resources to make these

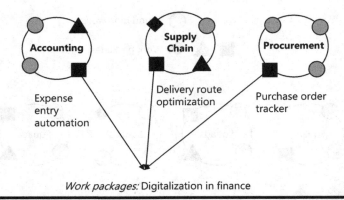

Work packages: Digitalization in finance

Figure 5.6 Defining common change requirements to define work packages across functions.

work packages a reality. These resources mean both human effort and investment allocation so the prioritization decision should be related to the most urgent and impactful requirement (Figure 5.6).

In conclusion, we can say that reversing the strategic design flow where every priority is driven from valid stakeholder needs, verified by the insight gathered around the organization allows focusing on where it matters. Another dimension is the diversification of breakthrough work packages from foundational tasks. This differentiation enables shifting thinking from sticking to daily and usual tasks toward questioning what initiatives can help to bring the company through breakthrough advancement. In this way, the daily tasks are reduced and minimized in time, focusing more on innovative initiatives.

5.6 Workflows

The last enabler is to set a governance structure within the department so that the workflows can be executed effectively. After the company strategy is designed and communicated, the teams start working on the 90-day priorities. Many of the work packages that are described above require more than one squad or department to be involved, and some even require teams to continuously connect and collaborate. Although agile systems make the within team workflow and collaboration very systematic, a company-wide workflow management platform is required to make sure that the same wholesomeness also applies out of the squad.

Workflow platform means the organizational system to manage internal demand and supply of work. Unfortunately, this definition may not resemble much because although the model is highly critical, very few companies are mature enough to use it and realize the related benefits. However, there is one simple form of these workflows that is rather common; which is the IT ticketing system. This ticketing system is used when a business unit requests software development from the IT team. The demanding unit enters all the details related to the system development requirement in a form and submits it to the IT department. The receiving end reviews the demand and approves the ticket if the development is going to be done and enters an estimated time of completion in some cases. Within this timeframe, the business unit can track the status of the ticket from this workflow management system.

Now imagine this mechanism for any sort of internal demand and supply relation within units. A common use case when I realized the benefits of applying was with legal departments. The number of legal experts in a company are scarce and act as a central center of excellence. Due to this centralized structure and limited number of experts, and due to many different departments' inflowing demands, sometimes the work goes beyond the responding limit. When the workflow mechanism was introduced, the demands for legal advice started to be entered with more structure and details, and the legal advisors started to manage the inflow more effectively. In addition, the legal advisors started entering the expected time of completion to the inquiry demands and the related business unit knew approximately how long it would take to get a response.

When the model is up and running, there is another level of governance which pays off very well, which are the service-level agreements (SLAs). This term is generally used not within company processes but when there is an external party, and when that party is responsible for providing a service to a unit. The SLA is a written commitment from the external provider, promising certain quality targets for the service to be provided. Common examples are delivery companies committing to hours of delivery or contact centers committing to the ratio of first-line resolutions. So we take things to another level here and offer to implement the same sort of agreement between parties who have continuous interdepartmental workflow. An example can be between sales and pricing teams; frequently members of these two have a long-lasting quarrel, the sales specialist is eager to declare the lowest price to the customer and close the deal as soon as possible where the pricing specialist has to make sure the right pricing that ensures profitability. In an applied case we have settled an SLA stating what minimum information the form coming from sales should include and the average time a pricing response should take.

Application of this method is beneficial from different perspectives; first of all, there is transparency within units that do not operate under the same roof but have ongoing business relationships. Second, stating the SLAs with expected time of response or required information clarified the expectations from another department, on top, showing the demands on the queue and the business of the receiving unit helped to create empathy toward an unknown team. Lastly, it creates efficiency due to the eliminated time and effort spent on tracking the status for an open query or blocked incomplete entries which created a lot of back-and-forth transactions.

the benefits they have traced overall through the book.

Chapter 6

Conclusion

Through this book I have tried to cover all three stages of agility, starting from
project agility, evolving toward organizational agility and completing with business
agility. As you may agree, even in the initial stage of project agility, there are substantial benefits that companies can start realizing instantly, and I may say that many
multinationals around me are experiencing.

And when you have read the chapters about organizational and then business
agility, I guess you have realized how much time and effort this transformation
implies and how much more dedication is required when compared to other sorts
of change efforts through the last two to three decades. But it also means you have
read through the wide range of immense benefits to the organizations from business,
customer and employee perspectives.

Seeing what it takes, the companies which are willing to embark on this journey
should define their goals first. Through the last years of my career, due to scarcity
of agile experts, I had a wonderful opportunity to meet dozens of leaders from
companies from a wide range of sectors and tried to assist them with their transformation. I noticed one main point: some companies initiate this effort to be trendy,
to look fancy as the first agile company in their sector, to apply to some sorts of
awards, those companies' journeys did not bring exponential benefits. I have heard
back from them saying they have launched the model however – everything is
operating the same – in the organization. So much time and effort are invested
and so many promises are made to the employees that a wind backward truly is a
pity and waste.

On the other hand, I also cooperate with companies who are enthusiastic about
the change, the leaders know and truly accept that their positioning will never be
the same, the employees listen to the transformation thinking that it's too good to

DOI: 10.1201/9781003268437-6

be true. Those companies really successfully launch and immediately start realizing the benefits that we have covered all through the book.

So accepting the business management will never be the same again, take ownership of the change and make sure you enjoy the ride.

References

1. **5 Phases of Project Management** https://project-management.com/project-management-phases/
2. **Project management skills** https://www.projectmanager.com/blog/project-management-skills
3. **Project timeline** https://www.businessbullet.co.uk/business-analysis/business-analysis-involvement-through-the-project-lifecycle/
4. **Agile manifesto** https://agilemanifesto.org/history.html
5. **Agile manifesto** https://blog.humphreys-assoc.com/agile-manifesto/
6. **Agile values** https://www.scrumalliance.org/resources/agile-manifesto
7. **Minimum viable product** http://www.syncdev.com/minimum-viable-product/
8. **VUCA** https://usawc.libanswers.com/faq/84869
9. **Agile project management benefits** https://www.villanovau.com/resources/project-management/the-use-of-agile-project-management-is-increasing/
10. **Organizational structure** https://www.mckinsey.com/business-functions/organization/our-insights/the-five-trademarks-of-agile-organizations
11. **Layers** https://www2.deloitte.com/content/dam/Deloitte/us/Documents/human-capital/us-spans-and-layers-for-the-modern-organization-2020.pdf
12. **Attrition effect** Connell, A. O. & Phillips J.J. (2012). Chapter 1. In Managing employee retention: A strategic accountability approach. Essay. Elsevier.
13. **Origins of agility** Wouter, A. & De Smet, A. & Murarka, M. & Collins L. (2015) McKinsey Publishing https://www.mckinsey.com/business-functions/organization/our-insights/the-keys-to-organizational-agility
14. **Origins of agility** Prats M.J. et al. (2018). Organizational Agility, IESE Business School, University of Navarra and Oliver Wyman Publishing https://media.iese.edu/research/pdfs/ST-0477-E.pdf
15. **Leadership in VUCA environment** Horney, N. & Passmore B. & O'Shea, T., Leadership (2009). Leadership Agility: A Business Imperative for a VUCA World. People & Strategy. http://luxorgroup.fr/coaching/wp-content/uploads/Leadership-agility-model.pdf
16. **Performance Management in VUCA World** Bennett, N., & Lemoine, G. J. (2014). *What a difference a word makes: Understanding threats to performance in A VUCA world. Business Horizons.* Elsevier, Kelley School of Business Indiana University.
17. **VUCA examples** Bennett, N., & Lemoine, G. J. (2014). What VUCA Really Means for You. *Harvard Business Review Magazine.*
18. **Organizational agility survey** Prats, M.J. et al. (2018) Organizational Agility, IESE Business School, University of Navarra and Oliver Wyman Publishing https://media.iese.edu/research/pdfs/ST-0477-E.pdf

19. **Organizational agility definition** https://www.scaledagileframework.com/organizational-agility/
20. **Product owner** https://www.scrum.org/resources/what-is-a-product-owner
21. **Agile roles** Jacobs, P. & Schalatmann, B. & Mahadevan, D. (2017). ING's Agile Transformation. *McKinsey Quarterly.*
22. **Liberating structures** http://www.liberatingstructures.com/
23. **Scrum** https://www.scrumalliance.org/about-scrum/definition
24. **Sprint** https://www.visual-paradigm.com/scrum/what-is-sprint-in-scrum/
25. **Kanban** https://www.agilealliance.org/glossary/kanban
26. **Fluid resources** Rotich, J., & Okello, B. (2019). The Effect of Resource Fluidity on Strategic Agility Among Universities: Case of Masinde Muliro University of Science and Technology. *The Strategic Journal of Business & Change Management.* 6(2).
27. **Enterprise agility** https://businessagility.institute/learn/enterprise-agility/
28. **Industry 4.0** Marr, B. (2018). What is Industry 4.0? Here's A Super Easy Explanation For Anyone. *Forbes Magazine.* September 2018 Issue.
29. **Robotic Process Automation** Boulton, C. (2018). What is RPA? A revolution in business process automation. *CIO Magazine.* September 2018 Issue.
30. **Internet of Things** Clarck, J. (2016). What is the Internet of Things (IoT)? *IBM Blogs*, https://www.ibm.com/blogs/internet-of-things/what-is-the-iot/
31. **Growth mindset** Dweck, C. (2016). What Having a "Growth Mindset" Actually Means. *Harvard Business Review.* January 2016 Issue.
32. **T shaped Profiles** Sharma, G. (2018). Which Letter-shaped employee you are? Linkedin.
33. **Backcasting Method** Holmberg, John & Robèrt, Karl-Henrik. (2000). Backcasting – A framework for strategic planning. *International Journal of Sustainable Development & World Ecology.* 7.
34. **Backcasting definition** https://en.wikipedia.org/wiki/Backcasting
35. **Spiral model** Nrip, Nripesh & Behl, Gunjan. (2012). A Study of Agile Software Development Model. I. 195.
36. **Financial control** https://corporatefinanceinstitute.com/resources/knowledge/finance/financial-controls/
37. **Objectives and key results** Niven, P. R., & Lamonte, B. (2017). *Objectives and key results: Driving focus, alignment, and engagement with okrs.* John Wiley & Sons.
38. **Marketing** Botha, J. Dr. (1998). Introduction To Marketing. Juta Academic.
39. **Market research** https://www.investopedia.com/terms/m/market-research
40. **Cost based pricing** Wood, M. S. (1985). *Cost analysis, cost recovery, marketing, and fee-based services: A guide for the health sciences librarian.* The Haworth Press.
41. **Design thinking** Uebernickel, F., Jiang, L., Brenner, W., Pukall, B., Naef, T., & Schindlholzer, B. (2020). *Design thinking: The handbook.* World Scientific.
42. **Design thinking process** Brenner, W. & Uebernickel, F. (2018). *Design thinking for innovation: Research and practice.* Springer.
43. **Marketing communication** Koekemoer, L., & Bird, S. (2004). *Marketing communications.* Juta Academic.
44. **Personalization** Russell, Smith, P.R. & Zook, Z. (2020). *Marketing communications: Integrating online and offline integration, customer engagement, and analytics technologies.* KoganPage.
45. **Personas** France, H. (2020). How To Create Personas For Marketing In 2021. Digital Agency Network Blog https://digitalagencynetwork.com/how-to-create-personas-for-marketing/

46. **Portfolio prioritization** Hill, S., Ettenson, R., & Tyson, D. (2005). Achieving the Ideal Brand Portfolio. *MITSloan Management Review*. Magazine Winter 2005.

47. **Omni channel** Kotarba, M. (2016). New factors inducing changes in the retail banking customer relationship management (CRM) and their exploration by the fintech industry. *Foundations of Management*. 8(1), 69–78.

48. **Customer Experience** https://www.prnewswire.com/news-releases/new-research-from-dimension-data-reveals-uncomfortable-cx-truths-300433878.html

49. **Premium based compensation** Chung, D.J. (2015). How to Really Motivate Salespeople. *Harvard Business Review*. Magazine April 2015.

50. **Hard selling** Connick, W. (2019). Understanding Different Sales Approach Methods. *The Balance Careers*. https://www.thebalancecareers.com/types-of-sales-approaches-2917015

51. **Persuasion in selling** Bova, T. (2019). 26 Sales Statistics That Prove Selling Is Changing. *SalesForce*. https://www.salesforce.com/blog/15-sales-statistics/

52. **Ratcheting quotas** Chung, D.J. (2015). How to Really Motivate Salespeople. *Harvard Business Review*. Magazine April 2015.

53. **Value based selling principles** Alfred, S. https://blog.hubspot.com/sales/value-based-selling

54. **Word of mouth** https://www.nielsen.com/us/en/insights/article/2012/consumer-trust-in-online-social-and-mobile-advertising-grows/

55. **Lines of defense** IAA Position Paper. (2013). The Three Lines Of Defense In Effective Risk Management And Control. The Institute of Internal Auditors. January 2013.

56. **Response time vs customer satisfaction** Sabur, V. F., & Simatupang, T. M. (2015). Improvement of customer response time using Lean Office. *International Journal of Services and Operations Management*. 20(1), 59.

57. **Internal audit** Sabuncu, B. (2017). Internal control and audit relation in corporations. *Economics and Social Sciences Journal of C.U.* 18(2).

58. **Second line of defense** Astley, P. et al. (2020). *Modernizing the three lines of defense model An internal audit perspective*. Deloitte.

59. **Internal audit** All in a Day's Work a Look at the Varied Responsibilities of Internal Auditors. Global TheIIA. www.theiia.org

60. **Audit process** Leftheris, J.M. The Audit Process presentation notes. www.theiia.org

61. **New ways of audit** Narayanan, R. Mind Over Matter: Implementing Agile Internal Audit Content by Deloitte. *Wall Street Journal*. August 2018.

62. **New ways of audit** Ho, J. & Li, T.W. (2019). Agile Internal Audit. KMPG paper.

63. **Operations strategy** Rolstadaas, A., Hvolby, H.-H. & Falster, P. (2008). IFIP International Federation for Information Processing, Volume 257, Lean Business Systems and Beyond, Tomasz Koch, ed. Springer.

64. **Workflows** Nafie, Faisal. (2013). The Role of Processes Re-Engineering and Workflow In The Transformation Of E-Government. *International Journal of Computational Engineering Research*. 3, 19–26.

65. **Workflow levels** Scheer, August-Wilhelm & Nüttgens, Markus. (2000). ARIS Architecture and Reference Models for Business Process Management. LNCS.

66. **Kanban Toyota** https://www.atlassian.com/agile/kanban

67. **Work in progress** https://www.scrum.org/resources/blog/limiting-work-progress-wip-scrum-kanban-what-when-who-how

68. **Time cycles** https://www.atlassian.com/agile/kanban

69. **Dropped calls** https://www.callcentrehelper.com/define-lost-calls-89049.htm

70. **Six sigma** Salah, S.; Rahim, A. & Carretero, J.A. (2010) The Integration of Six Sigma and Lean Management. *International Journal of Lean Six Sigma*. 1(3).

71. **Kanban roadblocks** https://berriprocess.com/en/how-to-drive-process-improvement-with-kanban/
72. **Work estimation methods** https://www.productplan.com/glossary/fibonacci-agile-estimation
73. **Agile culture** Laloux, F. (2016). *Reinventing Organizations: A Guide to Creating Organizations Inspired by the Next Stage in Human Consciousness*. Nelson Parker.
74. **Teal organization** Laloux, F. (2016). *Reinventing Organizations: A Guide to Creating Organizations Inspired by the Next Stage in Human Consciousness*. Nelson Parker.
75. **Three breakthroughs of teal organizations**, Laloux, F. (2016). *Reinventing Organizations: A Guide to Creating Organizations Inspired by the Next Stage in Human Consciousness*. Nelson Parker.
76. **Ikigai** https://en.wikipedia.org/wiki/Ikigai
77. **VACC** Lurie, M. & Tegelberg, L. (2019). *The new roles of leaders in 21st century organizations*. McKinsey & Company Organization Blog.
78. **HIPPO effect** Kaushik, A. (2007). *Web Analytics: An hour a day*. Wiley.
79. **Purpose driven organization** O'Brien, D., Main, A., Kounkel, S. & Stephan, A.R. (2019). *Purpose is everything: How brands that authentically lead with purpose are changing the nature of business today*. Deloitte Article.

Index

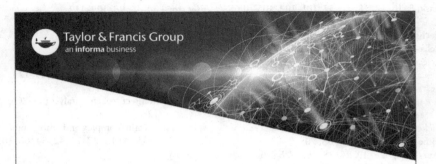

Printed in the United States
by Baker & Taylor Publisher Services

Printed in the United States
by Baker & Taylor Publisher Services